CLEARING INDIA'S AIR

Solutions to the Air Pollution Crisis

Naresh Garg

To the millions of Indians whose lives are cut short each year by polluted air - may this book be a call to arms to reclaim your right to breathe freely.

To the children across India whose childhood has been tainted by toxic skies - may the solutions within these pages help build a future of blue skies and healthy lungs.

To the activists, scientists, and concerned citizens working tirelessly on the frontlines against air pollution - your tireless efforts have inspired this book's vision of cleaner cities and villages.

To Mother Nature, whose resplendent bounty and life-sustaining atmospheric cycles we have polluted - may this work be a modest offering towards restoring balance.

To my family, whose unwavering love and support gave me strength during the long journey of this book - your encouragement is the oxygen that allowed these words to breathe.

To India, my beloved homeland - it is my greatest hope that the knowledge within catalyzes the transformative change needed to return your skies to pristine azure.

The air we breathe touches every pore of our being and every fiber of our body. It is the first nourishment we take, straight from the providers of life.

DR. T.C. DHARMARAJ, INDIAN ENVIRONMENTAL SCIENTIST

CONTENTS

FOREWORD

When I first began studying air pollution in the early Age, India was still perceived as a rising economic power largely unshackled from environmental concerns. The country's development ambitions took precedence, while pollution controls were an afterthought at best.

How swiftly the tides have shifted. Today, toxic air has emerged as an existential crisis that threatens the health, prosperity, and very future of the nation itself. No longer can India's pollution problem be swept under the rug or dismissed as a negligible sacrifice en route to modernity. The successively worse air quality seasons year after year have shattered that illusion.

The pages of this book lay bare the harsh realities. Every year, over a million Indians are dying prematurely from polluted air. Childhood asthma and adult lung disease rates have skyrocketed. Billions upon billions are squandered in economic losses as health costs mount and productivity craters. Verdant agricultural regions get shrouded in dense smog from crop burning. Even our ancient architectural marvels like the Taj Mahal are being disfigured by hazardous particulate matter.

Most tragically, the burden weighs heaviest on the most vulnerable segments of society - the rural poor, waste-pickers foraging in landfills, residents languishing near industrial clusters. A privileged few may be able to buy temporary reprieves with air purifiers or escapes to hill stations. But the harsh truth is that there is no insulation from the pervasive kreplach of polluted air that is India's new normal.

And yet, for all this book's sobering data points and illumination of the crisis's root causes, it is not an foreclosure of gloom. Rather, it charts an actionable pathway forward with sector-specific solutions, policy prescriptions, financing models, and multi-stakeholder partnerships to bend the curve. It provokes by underscoring that India's development need not come at the cost of healthy air, but in fact depends on it.

The road will demand immense willpower, cooperation, and resources. Modernizing vehicle standards, transitioning to clean energy and industrial production, reducing emissions from residential combustion - these are not easy feats. Deeply entrenched interests, bureaucratic inertia, and public apathy all loom as formidable headwinds.

But what this book makes resoundingly clear is that India has reached an existential juncture. The choice is between resigning our children to inherit a perpetual dystopia of breathless suffering and haze-shrouded cities unfit for human flourishing. Or we can summon the foresight and courage to reverse our catastrophic ecological trajectory.

The path illuminated in these pages is, simply put, the only one that can preserve Indian civilization long into the future. I implore every reader - government leader, corporate executive, ordinary citizen - to embrace the clarion call and join the life-or-death struggle to return India's skies to blue.

Anything less than an unwavering national commitment is to introduce toxic backsliding as the new norm. That is an inheritance too bleak to apprehend and too unforgiving to accept. Let this book mark the catalyzing moment when the era of polluted denial ended, and India chose clean air as the only way forward.

PREFACE

The air we breathe is a basic human necessity that is often taken for granted. Yet for millions of Indians, the struggle to find clean air is a harsh daily reality. India's air pollution crisis has reached catastrophic levels, casting a thick blanket of toxic smog over cities and rural areas alike. The consequences are dire - millions of premature deaths each year, rising rates of respiratory and cardiovascular diseases, and untold economic losses.

This book aims to shed light on India's unfolding pollution disaster through a comprehensive examination of the causes, impacts, and potential solutions. From the smoky plumes of crop burning to the dense traffic fumes on city roads, we explore the myriad sources fueling this public health emergency. We delve into the government policies enacted so far, analyzing their successes and failures. And crucially, we chart a path forward with evidence-based strategies and the investments required to reclaim blue skies.

Drawing on extensive research, data analysis, and insights from experts and frontline activists, this book serves as both a wake-up call and a beacon of hope. For too long, the issue of air pollution has been viewed through the short-sighted lens of industrialization versus environment. This book seeks to reframe the narrative, showcasing how improving air quality is not just an environmental imperative but an economic and moral one as well.

India has the potential to become a global leader in sustainable development and pollution control. But it will take concerted action at all levels - from government and industry to civil society and individual citizens. The road will not be easy, but the stakes could not be higher. Our children's futures - their ability to breathe freely without risking disease - depend on the choices we make today.

This book is a call to arms, imploring all stakeholders to come together and make the great smog of India a relic of the past. Only through collective action and an unwavering commitment can we restore azure skies as our national inheritance. The time to act is now.

CHAPTER 1 - TOXIC SKIES: INDIA'S UNFOLDING POLLUTION DISASTER

1.1 Choking in Plain Sight

Winter descends with a shroud of dread for Aarohi's family in inner city Lucknow. As the innocent 8-year old steps out for school bundled in sweaters, she breaks into coughs inhaling the bitter cold air. Her lungs have weathered many seasons of eye-stinging smog and incessant hacking, but this year the tiny smoke and dust particles suspended feel especially hard to escape.

Two months back, her father Mukesh, an electrician, had already swapped their family scooter for a 2nd hand car, hoping to protect little Aarohi from road dust and fumes during long commutes to school. The scooter ride would leave her wheezing through a stuffy nose by the time they reached home in the evenings.

But now, even within their gritty neighborhood, foul fumes pervade from passing trucks, the overflowing garbage dump down the street and constantly humming diesel generators supplying erratic mains power.

"Get the nebulizer quick" - Mukesh shouts out to his wife Sunita as Aarohi struggles to catch her breath on the walk back from school.

The pediatrician had warned them to expect a dire winter this year as crop burning smoke travels from neighboring states.

Sunita rummages through the medicine shelf past empty inhalers and cough syrup bottles to retrieve the nebulizer kit. Aarohi braces for the bitter asthma medicine to work its magic so her airways open up again for precious gulps of air.

In the panicked moments as they watch their only daughter gasp, Mukesh and Sunita feel alternately angry and helpless about not being able to protect her from the pollution scourge tightening its grip on their neighborhood, city and the entire Indo-Gangetic belt.

"I wish we could give her a mask that filtered everything out" signs Sunita. But the N95 was impractical for an 8-year old to wear through long school days. Moving homes was an impossible dream financially. All they could do was limit her outdoor time, keep nebulizer refills stocked and hope the skies cleared up after winter.

As Aarohi's breathing eases into a wheezy rhythm, the glint returns to her eyes. But Mukesh and Sunita cannot shake off the dread of what permanent damage awaits her lungs with each passing exposure-filled season, wondering if their little girl would ever get to play carefreely under clean blue skies.

1.2 Creeping Trends

Stories like Aarohi's are distressingly commonplace now across urban India. Latest satellite analysis comparing air quality over the past decade reveals that between 2010 to 2020, average nationwide particulate pollution has risen over 65% to dangerous levels.

Every year as winter approaches, a palpable tension grips cities as if bracing for battle. Sure enough, the months of October to February engulf the entire Indo-Gangetic plains belt in a public health nightmare - as particulate matter, nitrous oxides, sulphur dioxide and black carbon emissions explode.

In the capital New Delhi, daily air quality index (AQI) readings categorised as 'severe' or 'hazardous' now prevail for 4-5 months annually on average when PM2.5, PM10 and NOx particulates hit highs of 8 to 10 times the safe limits. What is unfathomable is millions have no choice but to continue living, working and commuting amidst this toxic smoke, often miles from any air quality monitoring station.

Delhi no longer remains an outlier. Satellite imagery now reveals previously deemed 'cleaner' cities in South India such as Bangalore, Chennai, Hyderabad and even tier-2 industrial cities like Kanpur, Lucknow, Patna hurtling down pollution curves to rival North India's worst.

In Chennai for instance, overall pollution load has risen 45% in just a half decade while Bangalore fared only slightly better at 12% deterioration as vehicular explosion outpaced infrastructure. Even tourism and wellness haven Goa now belies its paradise image with several urban pockets violating safe annual PM2.5 thresholds.

Clearly decades of unrestrained urbanization and fossil-fuelled growth have engulfed the entire subcontinent in unsafe air, making stories like Aarohi's the tragic new normal.

1.3 Killer Particulates

Why are microscopic particles like PM2.5, a fraction of the width of human hair, so hazardous when inhaled? Their tiny size enables deepest penetration straight into the lungs. Prolonged exposure is linked to increased risk of stroke, lung cancer, asthma attacks, irregular heartbeat, brain damage and even birth defects.

The World Health Organization stipulates an annual safe level of 5 micrograms per cubic metre. Yet recent analysis indicates over 480 million Indians currently breathe toxic air with concentration exceeding 100 while millions more face 50-100.

When PM2.5 levels hit 500-900 µg/m3 as is now common in North India from December to February, health impacts emerge within days to weeks especially for the vulnerable. Instances of stroke and heart attacks spike almost instantly from the inflammation and constricted blood flow.

Lung functionality loss becomes more irreversible each season as the finest silica particles scar delicate alveolar tissue. Children exposed lose vital development years, suffering damage akin to heavy smokers. Cancer risks cascade over years of exposure.

Ozone and nitrous oxides likewise penetrate deep, corroding lung lining fluid and making breathing progressively laborious. Toxic polyaromatic hydrocarbons attach to PM2.5 envelopes to disturbing effect.

While danger peaks in winter, festering levels of particulates, nitrogen and sulfur oxides, carbon soot, construction dust and industrial exhausts now prevail year-round across most Indian cities, towns and even rural areas.

Nowhere is truly safe for the body from this constant toxicity assault. Stories like Aarohi's are becoming tragically commonplace as pollution trends deteriorate unchecked.

1.4 Haunted Horizons

Stepping out on his apartment balcony with a cup of evening tea, retired banker MR Joshi is momentarily enthused seeing the golden sun rays scattered in the horizon through the silhouettes of Neem trees nearby.

As he looks further across the city landscape, his mood sinks. Buildings just half a kilometer away fade out behind a opaque, sickly yellow pall of smog hanging low, as if shrouded by a curtain. "We seem to inhabit the set of a dystopian doomsday movie" he sighs aloud.

Joshi feels unusually fatigued just gazing at the soupy air, as though the heavy metal toxins permeating it take psychic toll having already conquered the physical environment. The spectral haze leads him to discard plans for his habitual evening stroll to the neighborhood park.

But holing up indoors provides only brief respite from the all pervasive pollution as AQI meters placed around his living room confirm. Particulates seep through closed windows and fine enough to penetrate masks with casual use. His grandson's nebulizer whirrs constantly these days. Eyes itch.

Mr Joshi feels strangely bereft, almost depressed. The city's contours and skyline he had grown to love over 45 years now remain obscured for months by the opaque shroud. "Will we ever see clear horizons again? Or are permanently doomed to this haunted existence!" he wonders despondently.

While pollution health risks preoccupy Joshi, at deeper level the visual erasure of familiar vistas also seems to erase his very sense of belonging and roots in a place rendered nearly unrecognizable. He yearns for azure skies and crisply visible treelines of the Lucknow he once knew. Nothing less would suffice for the soul.

1.5 Alarming New Norms

Frontline doctors are witnessing an unprecedented epidemic of pollution-related illnesses ranging from lung functionality loss to heart attacks and strokes across age groups.

Especially severe impacts emerge amongst residents of cities long afflicted by toxic air like Delhi, Lucknow, Kanpur but also fast degrading tier 2 cities like Patna, Chandigarh, Ranchi where mitigation measures lag.

With PM2.5 levels spiking to 8-10X safe limits through winter months, instances of emergency hospitalization for respiratory distress, breathlessness and hypoxia are rising. Paediatric and geriatric wards typically overflow with little ones and elderly battling aggravated asthma, chronic bronchitis or pneumonia attacks.

Cancer wards are also seeing surge in lung cancer instances alongside other forms with direct correlation to prolonged toxin exposure from studies. Alarming case clusters around industrial belts are just beginning to emerge now.

Even more worrying is heightened risk of heart attacks, irregular heartbeat and strokes from inflammation and constricted blood flow, with some reports calculating incidence spiking 20% year on year even amongst relatively younger adults in severely polluted cities.

Doctors confirm organ function deterioration and tissue scarring among repeated longtime residents of toxic air zones, leading to accelerated aging. Patients complain of perpetual weakness, nausea and headaches emerging as early as late October in anticipation of winter air trauma.

Skin infections, allergies and vitamin D deficiency linked to avoiding sunlight have also seen sharp uptick. Clearly the era of 7 million+ premature deaths from air pollution paints a dystopian picture for India with medical norms altered dramatically for the worse.

1.6 Life Cut Short

The devastating health impacts are hitting hardest amongst vulnerable groups - children like Aarohi who lose out on formative lung development during key growth years. Asthma, risk of heart disease and cancer cascade into their adulthood.

Daily wage laborers also shoulder an outsized burden, with limited access to protective gear. Whether digging roads, ferrying construction material, cleaning sewers or loaders at landfills, they inhale the most noxious road dust and industrial fumes.

Auto and taxi drivers similarly have little respite from traffic emissions penetrating cabins for 11-12 hour shifts, reporting chronic coughs and breathing issues in just a few years.

Traffic police at smog dense intersections bear the brunt - with studies proving they inhale toxin loads akin to smoking 50 cigarettes a day! Heart attacks have caused early retirement and worse.

Homeless people are also brutally exposed to both day and night pollution with limited escape. Street dwellers are fighting recurrent respiratory diseases.

According to medical journal Lancet's comprehensive analysis, air pollution exposure causes an estimated 1.7 million premature deaths nationally per year as of 2019 with number rising as trends deteriorate. Most never make headlines as slow acting malignancy.

But lives are being cut short nonetheless - whether 8 year olds robbed of clean air or 40 year old labourers robbed of breath itself. Pollution discriminates by class in who lives longest, but ultimately catches up with even the privileged Denis in cities signalling drastic policy action needed

1.7 Winter Peaks

While pollution remains dangerously high year-round across Indian cities, the winter months of October through February see runaway spikes as a confluence of seasonal factors conspire to create a toxic peak.

As temperatures drop, falling air pressure and lighter winds allow particulate matter, vehicular fumes, industrial emissions and other gases to hang heavy near the earth's surface for longer duration. Hazy grey skies become the norm across Northern plains.

October coincides with massive crop residue burning across Punjab, Haryana and UP farms which releases plumes of smoke containing particulate matter, CO_2, NOX travelling as far as Delhi NCR triggering health emergency conditions within days. Stubble plumes alone can drive up pollution curves exponentially.

During winters, rural firewood and dung-based household heating needs rise, leaving villages blanketed in thick smog daily from makeshift earthen stoves or 'chulhas' often housed indoors as well due to cold. Likewise, as urban slum dwellers huddle around night fires for warmth amidst cramped on-road tents or hutments, the poorly combusted fumes add concentrated dose of toxins while their immunity also drops due to cold.

Frigid temperatures attract more fuel combustion from transportation and thermal power plants to address rising electricity demand. But slack environmental compliance means uncontrolled amounts of sulfur dioxide, nitrogen oxide and dangerous PM 2.5 billow out - boosting airshed toxicity levels manifold in just few weeks.

Construction project dust also surges in the rush to complete activities before winter. And December ushers annual calendar of religious events, festivals, weddings with extensive firecracker bursting and unregulated diesel generator usage across cities ignoring pollution fallouts in the revelry.

Ultimately the dangerous crescendo of human activity and seasonal effects reaches a tipping point from October to February every year - plunging the Indo-Gangetic belt especially into a notoriously lethal public health nightmare. The ambient air transforms into a veritable poison blanket for millions with infants, elderly and working poor suffering the most intense impact. But now, no one remains unscathed.

Words alone cannot capture the sheer dread cities now associate with the advent of winter. It is quite literally a battle for survival.

1.8 Rural Scourge

Urban hotspots understandably draw focus, but toxic air pollution remains very much a hinterland India plague as well. Unregulated small factories, brick kilns relying on dirty feeds, diesel generator sets, burning crop stubble on millions of farms, garbage fires and even household cooking release dangerous cocktail of PM2.5/10 particulates, NOx gases, SOx, black carbon and volatile compounds now identified as precursors even for fatal non-communicable diseases.

Yet monitoring remains minimal in rural areas while causing equally devastating health outcomes. IIT Kanpur's expansive bounded box modelling of air flows shows during peak crop burning months, many villages can rival cities in average pollution load. In mandis, fumes from truck exhausts and farm machineries envelop locals daily. Roadside suburbs fare worse. Diesel pumps dot thoroughfares in a chocking haze.

Farm soil quality is also getting affected by pesticide overuse and heavy metal deposition from industrial emissions - eventually entering crops and food chain. Bundelkhand's alarming arsenic contamination linked to coal power emissions matched Bangladesh levels per studies.

The worst impacts emerge among farmers directly inhaling residual crop burning smoke, unable to wear protective masks for long work days. Their immune health wears down after months of sequential paddy and wheat harvests amidst smouldering farmlands, causing lung inflammation issues to resurface year on year. Incidence and intensity of lung, sinus and skin cancers emerging around brick kilns and coal plants near farmlands is also generating concern based on anecdotal evidence.

Without better emissions compliance enforcing framework for rural zones, air pollution countryside could deteriorate to match toxic cities in coming years while ravaging critical food producing hamlets and socio-economically vulnerable communities most directly tied to the land. The fallouts warrant much greater spotlight.

1.9 Economic Drag

Alongside its devastating health impacts, air pollution also inflicts a monumental economic toll on India, with implications for reduced productivity, healthcare costs and lost livelihoods.

According to World Bank estimates, pollution cost the country an staggering $36 billion in 2013 alone, equal to around 1.3% of GDP solely considering welfare losses. As pollution has worsened since, present costs likely approach a whopping 3% of GDP in direct health expenditure and productivity declines as per Harvard Analysis.

Healthcare costs treating pollution-linked illness total nearly $28 billion annually already by conservative WHO estimates - set to rise further as respiratory ailments, cardiac conditions and cancers spike.

Plus there is the immense burden of out of pocket expenditure driving families into poverty. With public health infrastructure overwhelmed, the urban and rural poor have little choice but to turn to expensive private clinics and hospitals for respiratory and cardiovascular distress, risking penury.

Polluted air also triggers lost workforce productivity from increased sickness absenteeism to the tune of 17 million working days lost per year costing $6.5 billion as per reports. Add to this reduced cognitive functioning and learning outcomes affecting quality and output.

Plus India loses up to 50% of crop yield in the most air polluted pockets as wheat, rice, cotton and fruit harvests are hit by ozone exposure and acid rain effects of NOx, SOx emissions. This cuts deep socio-economically given 60% reliance on agriculture. There are signs of rural unrest brewing.

When Delhi schools were shut for a week in Nov 2019 amidst 'hazardous' air quality, vegetable seller Raju reported an 80% drop in revenue as office goers vanished. "People only venture out for essentials in this smog" he lamented. Stories like Raju's indicate the scale of commercial activity also affected.

Overall air pollution is a hugely risky economic liability in the making, set to slow India's aspirations for upper middle income prosperity without urgent redress. The need for action has never been more urgent

1.10 Social Burden

The air pollution crisis also has drastic social implications in terms of exacerbating inequality. The worst affected are from marginalized economic groups with limited access to healthcare, protective gear or other mitigating resources.

Children attending ramshackle roadside schools suffer far worse exposure and resultant lung impediments than well-off students studying safely indoors with air filters and purifiers.

A recent DDU College study of school children in Delhi confirms the class divide - finding lung capacity reduced by over 50% in kids from lower income colonies vis-a-vis under 20% amongst posh South Delhi. 84% kids in some peripheral resettlement areas had impaired lung function.

The trauma also impacts learning outcomes and future productivity between cohorts. Likewise slum clusters and on-road homeless living are engulfed in toxicity hotspots day and night with severest health consequences.

Even amongst salaried groups, blue collar workers, traffic police, cycle rickshaw drivers inhale higher direct doses without recourse. House help and guards equally affected.

Ultimately the air pollution crisis jeopardizes sustainable development goals by exacerbating health, economic barriers between rich and BPL citizens; while also gender-wise seeing women disadvantaged from domestic smoke exposure.

All considered, air pollution abetted inequality remains among the biggest social burdens and calls for universal access to mitigation resources alongside resolving the emissions crisis itself

1.11 Policy Spotlight

While China achieved a 30% urban PM2.5 reduction from 2013-2018 and London slashed particulates by over 80% within a decade since 1990's by targeting coal and diesel emissions, India's policy interventions remain still born or loosely enforced.

The National Clean Air Program launched in 2019 created a national framework for pollution abatement but lacks legal authority. City specific plans got delayed by slow data collection and disjointed efforts on electric mobility, public transit, green buffers etc.

Industrial stack monitoring requirements and BS VI vehicles standards signal intent on improving airshed carrying capacity but enacted without matching supply infrastructure. Thermal power emission norms ignore financing needs - requiring $15 billion for retrofits.

Crop stubble fines have failed to deter debt-ridden farmers from burning fields for quick clearance between wheat and paddy cycles. Subsidies on farm equipment exist but reach <5% growers thus far due to red tape while bans remain virtue signaling.

Air Acts handed pollution control boards quasi judicial powers to prosecute offenders but resources inadequate and convictions rare. Green tax levies on smoke spewing trucks and old diesel cars invented but hardly enforced or evasion proof.

In essence, India's good intent neutron ambitions for breathable cities remain hindered by bureaucratic inertia, weak synergies across central and state agencies, enforcement blind spots, absence of regional cooperation and near absent public consultation avenues.

With millions gasping and lives cut short prematurely, the need to leapfrog from symbolic aspirations to meaningful action on war footing around air pollution discourse has never been more urgent

* * *

CHAPTER 2 - NATIONAL STATE OF AFFAIRS: INDIA'S AIR EMERGENCY

2.1 - Deteriorating National Trends

The latest government analysis paints a gloomy picture of steeply deteriorating air quality across both particulate matter and gaseous emissions over the past decade.

Checking 287 continuous air monitoring stations spanning metro cities and smaller towns over 2015-2020 period, the findings are stark. As much as 63% of India now falls under 'poor', 'very poor' or 'severe' air quality zones on an annual average basis.

This implies over 180 million Indians inhabit severely affected areas just going by National Clean Air Program's lenient thresholds of exceeding 60 micro-gm/cubic meter for PM10 and 40 micro-gm/cubic meter for PM2.5 particles.

And these monitoring stations represent just preliminary indicative coverage for a country of India's size. Actual figures could likely be twice as worse.

What is deeply concerning for climate and health experts is the slope of pollution curve heading north despite economic disruptions from pandemic - indicating systemic and uncontrolled drivers like thermal power, industries, vehicular explosion outstripping mitigation efforts.

PM2.5 levels are found exceeding safe limits across all seasons, with peak spikes breaching upper limits of measurement scales across Delhi, Lucknow, Patna during winter months due to unfavorable meteorology and agricultural biomass burning.

Clearly the magnitude of India's cities plunging into toxic air emergency year after year now warrants urgent policy interventions on a sweeping scale if this public health and climate crisis is to be arrested.

2.2 - Regional Variations

Granular spatial analysis reveals that the Indo-Gangetic plains emerge most critically pollution affected from combined sources spanning vehicular emissions, industrial clusters, coal power plants and seasonal biomass burning.

This densely populated fertile river basin witnesses average regional PM2.5 levels spiking as high as 170 micro-gm/cubic meter in winters of 2021-22 as per CPCB - nearly 35 times the WHO limits. NO2, SO2 and carbon soot metrics mirror this.

Prolonged exposure to such concentrations year after year sets off time-bomb for cardiovascular and respiratory health crisis.

Southern coastal cities like Chennai, Visakhapatnam were previously deemed relatively cleaner. But latest readings indicate PM2.5, NOx thresholds being exceeded by 45-50% over last 5 years alone amidst exponential construction activity, traffic explosion and meteorology changes.

Even Mumbai, Pune which enjoyed sea breeze now record 'poor' air days during winter months due to rapid concretization and vehicle growth.

Likewise arid regions of Rajasthan show massive spikes in coarse particulates and dust loading crossed alarming thresholds for Jodhpur, Jaipur residents as construction debris mixes with sandstorms.

Essentially barring the high altitude Eastern Himalayas, no region seems insulated from the scourge of worsening air pollution - reiterating the need for urgent national action plan addressing customized local and regional issues simultaneously.

2.3 - Seasonal Peaks

While dangerously high pollution now prevails through much of the year, the winter months of October to February see runaway spikes as a confluence of seasonal factors conspire to create a toxic peak.

As temperatures drop across North India, falling air pressure and weaker wind systems allow vehicular fumes, industrial emissions and other gases to hang heavy near the earth's surface for longer duration. This leaves entire Indo-Gangetic plains engulfed in lung-choking smog for days on end.

October coincides with massive crop residue burning across Punjab, Haryana and UP farms which releases plumes of smoke containing hazardous particulate matter, CO_2, NOX, volatile gases - travelling as far as Delhi NCR and triggering health emergency conditions within days.

Likewise, spike in coal combustion, construction activity, festival season traffic in these months drastically reduces airshed carrying capacity to absorb emissions. 95% monitoring stations have reported 'poor', 'very poor' or 'severe' air quality spanning November to February based on Central Pollution Control analysis.

Southern cities relatively shielded from agricultural fires also record marked seasonal deterioration as winters slow wind circulation, worsen inversion effect for coastal regions too. Metro cities now routinely figure in global lists of most polluted cities ranking during winter months.

Essentially due to unfavorable meteorology and uncontrolled anthropogenic actions, the skies above much of India turn into an opaque toxic soup for nearly half the year with panic setting in among urban populations. The seasonal trend urgently warrants emissions regulations.

2.4 - City Hotspots

While national trends paint a worrying picture, granular city-wise and even neighborhood-level air quality analysis based on satellite sensors and AI reveal more dangerous pollution hotspots.

As expected, landlocked megacities like Delhi, Lucknow lead lists of most polluted cities globally based on average yearly and peak pollution metrics - indicating extremely congested traffic, proximity to crop burning, thermal plants etc.

Other emerging hotspots figure in satellite imaging include industrial belt cities like Kanpur, Korba with high density of coal power plants, factories and mining activity. Unregulated emissions here both degrade local air severely and also impact regional airshed.

Likewise smaller cities witnessing uncontrolled construction boom such as Patna, Raipur see high dust generation wrecking neighborhood air quality irreparably as construction debris and bare earth mixes dangerously with traffic fumes.

Coastal cities were previously insulated but now intense concretization of Chennai, Visakhapatnam sharply deteriorates micro-climate while trapping vehicular emissions locally too. Mumbai, Pune record 'poor' air days even in winter months.

Essentially barring very few cities, a dense toxic blanket now engulfs most Indian urban agglomerates year-round basis while villages remain oblivious to pollution load from biomass burning, crop residue fires, brick kilns etc.

With rising geographic spread, air pollution truly emerges as India's greatest environmental health hazard needing combined policy, technology and public action across cities, rural areas simultaneously

2.5 - Health Crisis Significance

Comparing India's pollution exposure severity with medical insights on associated morbidity and mortality makes clear this is no longer just an environmental concern but a full blown health emergency.

As per WHO, over 90% of India's population breathes annual average PM2.5 levels exceeding even lenient Indian safe limits of 40ug/m3. Actual exposure equals smoking almost a pack of cigarettes per day for adults as per Berkeley analysis.

At 1.67 million deaths, India rivals China in total lives lost prematurely due to toxic air as per 2021 Lancet report findings. But adjusting for population, India emerges the worst impacted globally with rate of life years lost exceeding crisis thresholds.

Like smoking 15 cigarettes a day, the pollution health tax destroys lung functionality starting childhood, impedes development. Pre-existing conditions also get aggravated exponentially across age groups.

The mortality figures approach severity of a multi year pandemic playing out silently but relentlessly. Yet policy discourse and health infrastructure remains ill equipped to diagnose or correlate formally pollution linked disease spread, economic loss and life expectancy shrinkage so far. That calls for course correction.

With air pollution now the largest environmental health risk nationally, experts believe tackling this has to become top governance priority before sustainable development itself comes under threat. Targeted reductions in PM2.5 concentrations to WHO limits can save millions of lives alongside climate gains. The time for action is now.

2.6 - International Comparisons

India fares significantly worse than not only developed countries having controlled urban air pollution but also regional peers like China, Malaysia, Indonesia - both in pollution curve trends and mortality health data.

Cities like Delhi, Varanasi and Patna have recorded peak winter days PM2.5 spikes of 986, 685 and 467 micro-gm/cubic meter respectively considered 'hazardous' as per global standards.

Compare this to London which touched a high of only 158 micro-gm/cubic meter in the historically worst year of air pollution signaling the gulf in severity facing India.

Likewise China has managed to reduce average national PM2.5 concentration from 58 micro-gm/cubic meter to 42 between 2013-2020 - a 28% improvement via systematic policies targeting coal plants, industry and vehicles.

India in contrast has deteriorated 65% in same period with average national PM2.5 levels rising from around 46 to 76. Similarly NOx trends mirror this divergence, indicating the critical lapses in India's emission control frameworks.

Even tropical region peers Malaysia, Thailand, Indonesia fare significantly better in WHO's latest urban air quality database underscoring the need for India to urgently arrest this public health crisis even faster than peers.

Essentially India now ranks consistently as hosting many of the world's most polluted capital cities in global indexes. With also higher share of population exposed, India must strategize pollution target reductions faster than developing country counterparts before environmental health linked economic costs also start compounding further

Key Takeaways

The extensive air quality analysis across seasons and regions makes it abundantly clear that barring few pockets, India suffers a pervasive public health emergency from toxic air spanning its villages, towns and cities.

This is no longer just an annual winter phenomenon for Northern states but a persisting year-round crisis amplified during October to February. Coastal cities once insulated are also now stricken.

Comparing pollution trends and attributable health impacts, India fares the poorest amongst major developing economies - facing mortality scales rivaling prolonged pandemics annually.

Essentially the economic aspirations for a $5 trillion economy could flounder if made to run this deadly pollution gauntlet that cuts lives short by a decade and more in affected zones.

With Indian cities occupying 22 of 30 most polluted slots globally, there is no hiding from the harsh truth regarding the state of affairs ranging from policy failures to data gaps.

What Indo-Gangetic belt faces is an human induced public health disaster necessitating nothing short of emergency national action to control key sources across energy, transport, construction, waste management before entire generations gets afflicted.

Tough decisions around sustainability roadmap confront policy makers. But an environmental health crisis of this magnitude must take precedence over dated development paradigms. There ought to be no bigger priority for government that guaranteeing clean air to breathe for its citizens.

CHAPTER 3 - SOURCES AND ROOT CAUSES: DIAGNOSING INDIA'S AIR EMERGENCY

3.1 Counting the Key Culprits

Granular source apportionment studies make clear that the following sectors represent the chief culprits behind the toxic air quality engulfing India's cities, towns and rural areas today:

Transport - Vehicular exhaust emissions are identified as the single biggest source contributor to urban air pollution, alone responsible for over 60% of PM2.5 and NOx load as per government audits. Causes range from highly polluting aging vehicle fleet running outdated emissions control technology to ineffective inspection and maintenance mechanisms allowing badly maintained vehicles to ply unfettered. Ultra-fine particulates from tire and brake wear adds to toxicity as congestion delays upgrades.

Thermal Power Plants - Coal-fired electricity generation facilities with concentrated capacities in the Indo-Gangetic belt have emerged among the notorious emitters of neurotoxic mercury, lung-inflaming SOx gases and carcinogenic particulate matter through unchecked effluents across industry life-cycle. Over 75% of India's power still sourced from coal, lacks mandatory flue gas scrubbers exacerbating regional health crisis.

Industries - Especially steel plants, metal smelters, oil refineries, paper mills located in dense clusters flout emission norms contributing to both localized pollution emergencies as well as regional haze storms. Monitoring gaps asunits game emissions inventory data reporting while oversight capacities remain understaffed to enforce compliance.

Agricultural biomass burning - Paddy straw residue incineration through open field fires across Punjab, Haryana etc in preparation for winter cropping adds dangerously high seasonal spike in particulates, NOx and SOx precursors. Combined with transportation and waste burning emissions, winter months see 4-5X safe pollution limits.

Construction activity - The infrastructure boom across India's urban and suburban centers suffers from weak dust control measures at project sites leading to extreme neighborhood level pollution from loose material mishandling and debris overflow adding to traffic dust and industrial particles settling as city smog.

Waste burning - Plastic, rubber, biomass and electronic waste fires, though smaller emission loads, massively choke local air quality with intense toxicity from furans, dioxins and metal vapors. Most urban or rural Indian neighborhoods lie engulfed amidst some unregulated waste fire or the other.

Essentially field insights reveal the enormity of the combined assault on breathable air from lack of emissions oversight across economic activities in the country - with policy failures and continued infra-energy expansion ambitions trumping public health security. It sets the stage for why citizens gasp helplessly amidst world's most polluted air.

3.2 Transport Tailpipe Trauma

On-road vehicles have emerged as the largest culprit group contributing over 60% of urban PM2.5 load in cities as per the Automotive Research Association of India.

A host of factors conspire to turn transportation emissions into the chief toxin diminishing urban air quality and public health.

First, despite Bharat Stage VI upgrade, the overall passenger vehicle fleet mix remains outdated with poorly maintained heavy diesel vehicles including trucks, tractors and buses constituting bulk of emissions. Their outdated or revoked technology lacking emissions control equipment releases thick soot. Ultrafine particulates are also produced from tire and brake wear.

Second, compliance and enforcement mechanisms governing vehicular fitness remain dismal. Pollution Under Control Centres suffer glaring integrity issues in testing protocols allowing failing vehicles to secure clearance certificates through fake passes. This lets smoke-spewing clunkers operate unchecked.

Likewise the broken fuel quality supply system of India means sulphur-laced diesel or petrol heightens toxicity of exhaust further reducing effect of any after-treatment systems present. Heavy metals get released while catalytic converters choke.

Third, near absent public transport access across cities coupled with policy thrust on road and flyover expansion has catalyzed private vehicular explosion minus commensurate parking, adhesion to lane discipline or controlled fleet modernization further conspiring to turn roads into linear pollution hotspots immersed in idling engine smoke. Heavy fossil fuel addiction retains stronghold.

Overall the combined impact from also Metro construction dust, overloaded trickers, raging summer road dust all coalesce into the 41% fraction of NCAP's blamed on mobile traffic - demanding major mobility reforms. Our urban transportation systems are at root of the tailpipe emissions trauma engulfing city skies and lungs

3.3 Thermal Power's Toxic Legacy

Coal-fired power plants have emerged as among the most notorious emitters of dangerous neurotoxic heavy metals like mercury, lung-inflaming Sulphur dioxide and Nitrogen oxide gases along with respirable carcinogenic particulate matter.

Latest compliance audits reveal the vast unchecked emissions footprint from Indian thermal power plants poisoning regional air shed, water bodies and even food chains in surrounding villages.

Fly ash ponds laden with arsenic, lead, chromium dot the power plant landscapes prone to accidents and leeching into crops. Entire coal lifecycle suffers from heavy metal contamination and fugitive dust emissions during material movement impacting local habitations.

But the most devastating impact emerges from outdated electrostatic precipitators, lacking flue gas desulfurization (FGD) systems for SOx capture and selective catalytic reduction (SCR) of NOx expulsions from ochre emissions stacks ochre - releasing thick chemical haze traveling hundreds of kilometers.

Result is ambient SO2 levels at times crossing 60 microgram per cubic meter against safe limits of 20, NO2 spikes surpassing 94 against norm of 40. Nearby soil, water and cow milk samples also reveal dangerous toxin levels pointing to elevated cancer risks for communities around power plants.

Essentially the untreated effluents from coal-centric electricity pose among the highest environmental health hazards. But opaque zoning regulations and reliance on faulty emissions self-reporting by generators means damage control remains least priority so far.

3.4 Industrial Cluster Hotspots

With economic liberalization, India has seen mushrooming of industrial hubs specializing in textiles, chemicals, paper, cement, steel and other high emissions sectors.

Prominent industrial corridors like Gurugram-Neemrana-Bhiwadi now house over 500 large and 5000 small scale highly polluting factories in just 25km radius!

Likewise Chhattisgarh power plants flanked by smelters, Vapi-Ankleshwar chemical belt and Howrah tanneries join the ranks of 7 Critically Polluted Industrial Areas flagged by CPCB itself.

Yet on ground audits reveal extensive monitoring gaps. Either units totally evade emissions compliance via missing chimneys, manipulation of automated logging sensors or disguising incineration as fuel use to game inventory data reports to regulators.

So while progressive minimum emission benchmarks exist on paper for dioxins, furans and other toxins, the actual discharge load remains obscure and severely exceeded as poisonous effluents choke adjoining habitations.

Cancer clusters, skin conditions, respiratory issues afflict laborers and villages around India's industrial clusters due to callous zoning buffers and reliance on self-reporting rather than verifiable emissions performance. Price of unbridled manufacturing growth without pollution accountability gets passed on nearby communities while profits remain privatized.

Essentially the roots of industrial cluster hotspots lie in oversight gaps especially from small facilities, expedited clearances tradeoff and opacity around actual effluent audits demanding urgent reforms.

3.5 Farm Fires: A Seasonal Scourge

While year-round pollution load from vehicles, industry and power plants haunt Indian cities, the months of October-November also bring a terrifying spike in particulates and gases from raging farm fires across north India.

Over 100,000 stubble burning incidents are recorded annually despite bans contributing anywhere from 12% to even 46% of Delhi's winter pollution load making it the worst season for exposure.

Essentially paddy straw residue incineration from mechanized harvesting in states like Punjab, Haryana and western UP coupled with seasonal humidity and wind patterns leads to dense smoke carrying PM2.5, CO2, NOX to blanket entire Indo-Gangetic belt within days in a choking health emergency.

Contributing factors include lack of monitoring capacity for detection especially inability of satellites to capture small scattered fires, dependence of farmers on residue burning for quick field clearance before next wheat cycle, debt constraints in financing happy seeders and general lack of scalable circular bio-economy models for crop waste valorization currently - though alternatives exist on paper.

The harassment of penal actions against smallholder farmers also diminishes deterrence, requiring a behavioral change approach but current top down directives lack nuance.

Overall the explosive combination of legislative toothlessness, socio-economic limitations and administrative lag has allowed the seasonal scourge of farm fires to rage annually despite blanket bans - demanding urgent multi-dimensional interventions reconciling sustainability, livelihoods and public health

3.6 Choked Construction Economy

The infrastructure boom across India's metropolitan and tier 2 cities over last decade has been shadowed by a parallel surge in localized construction dust pollution emerging as third largest contributor overall.

Weak regulation of material handling protocols at project sites means extensive mishandling of loose cement, bricks, metal and concreting agents leaving the neighborhoods immersed in thick particulate smog round the clock - severely diminishing air quality.

Likewise debris from demolition waste left loosely managed adds toSuspend road dust clouds combining with industrial and fuel combustion byproducts already suffocating the air.

Hourly pollution spikes hence are recorded during peak construction periods itself adding over 40% to the dangerously high ambient particulate counts as per IIT analysis, but monitoring limitations lead to underestimation.

Cement factories, stone quarries, vehicular movement ferrying raw materials and labor colonies dotting urbanizing India's outskirts also join the pollution emission chain lacking mitigation efforts so far constituting construction economy's harmful legacy escaping spotlight thus far compared to vehicles, waste burning or stubble fires.

Essentially the diffused nature of builders' pollution footprint has allowed it to fly under the radar though choking residential zones already bearing brunt of multiple toxins sources now facing new threats to well-being from the thriving construction sector itself.

3.7 Waste Chokes Local Airsheds

While contributing smaller overall pollution load, instances of unregulated plastic, rubber, biomass and electronic waste fires massively choke local air quality with their high combustion intensity and toxic emissions.

Landfill sites overflowing with mixed garbage routinely catch fires, spewing dense toxic plumes containing dioxins, furans and metal vapours upon nearby urban slums, villages or habitations with minimal buffer zones followed. Delhi's recent Ghazipur landfill episode left schools shut.

Likewise frequent occurrence of waste tires, plastic, E-waste burning by ragpickers in urban peripheries to extract quick value poses extreme health hazard from vaporized heavy metals or cancer agents settling around densely packed neighborhoods lacking dust control.

Rural air quality also suffers from burning of agricultural leftovers, dung cakes or fuelwood amidst homesteads during winters again exposing women and infants to noxious indoor smoke daily lacking chimney ventilation.

While contributing relatively lower shares of overall city

pollution than say vehicles, the high toxicity impact from often overlooked decentralised waste burning or management practices makes it imperative to deploy mitigation efforts to at least protect vulnerable communities through scientifically planned buffer zones, toxicity sensors, sprinkler nets etc.

Essentially waste mismanagement represents a classic case of environmental externalities facing weakest, invisible sections of society while rest progresses economically. It demands accountability

3.8 Diagnoses of Root Causes

A few fundamental gaps emerge in diagnosis of the key triggers behind the losing battle for breathable air quality across India currently:

First, the unreconciled contradiction between the country's economic growth imperatives and environment sustainability planning being exposed now has trapped citizens gasping for clean air today in absence of foresight.

Unbridled infrastructure expansion, cold calculations prioritizing higher energy access over clean energy underlie the crisis now. But climate impacts or pollution breaching thresholds was never integrated in enterprise risk models.

Second, the utter inadequacy of environmental compliance and enforcement frameworks for point and non-point sources of emissions ranging from vehicle fitness to crop burning policing capacities facilitated the current breakdown.

Third, over-reliance on ambitious but impractical emission concentration standards rather than actual deterrence around real discharge loads from factories, utilities etc constrained impact. Outdated attitudes hampered.

Fourth, hyper-focus on end-of-pipe treatment schemes rather than facilitating transitions to sustainability solutions led to stranded assets. Be it power plant FGDs lacking operational viability or CNG vehicles needing robust refueling logistics.

Essentially the root causes behind India gasping amidst the world's worst air trace back to governance blind spots failing to instill circular economy thinking tying sustainability to economic priorities. Lost years demand catching up.

✻ ✻ ✻

CHAPTER 4 - GOVERNMENT ACTION SO FAR: HITS AND MISSES

4.1 Flagship Scheme - National Clean Air Program

The National Clean Air Program (NCAP) launched in 2019 remains India's hallmark initiative acknowledged even by UN agencies as a crucial policy response to the intensifying air pollution crisis nationally.

NCAP aims to create an overarching implementation framework for air quality management in the country - evolving collaborative multi-stakeholder action plans to meet ambitious 2024 targets.

These include a 20-30% reduction in hazardous particulate pollution across 122 identified non-attainment cities flouting safe standards. The targeted cities span Tier 1 metros, smaller urban agglomerates and even some rural zones.

Additionally it spotlights 28 industrial clusters, calls for expansion of monitoring network to rural India alongside bolstering capacity for data analytics, health impact studies and awareness drives.

However, three years from launch, NCAP remains crippled in efficacy owing to lack of legal authority, relying instead on fragmented state/city actions to achieve PM reduction without setting emissions caps leave alone deterrent fines regime.

There is negligible Central funding support for infrastructure or technology investments towards goals either. Continued reliance on traditional development projects like metro rails, highways or smart cities with higher pollution externalities also impedes progress.

Essentially while well-intentioned, NCAP currently resembles virtue signaling attempts around air quality consciousness than actual gamechanging governance reform spearheading adoption of next generation sustainability solutions at scale under unprecedented multi-department efforts.

The program warrants a 2.0 reboot as a scientifically steered national mission with renewed targets, bolstered capabilities, hard accountability metrics and most of all - greatly enhanced financing to catalyze public health impact aligned to polluter pay principle.

4.2 City Action Plans

Flowing from the National Clean Air Program, over a 100 cities have formulated City Action Plans unique to their local pollution sources and meteorology hotspots.

These localized plans aim to augment public transport infrastructure, operationalize real-time pollution hotspot mitigation technologies like smog-towers, expand green buffers along roads, deploy water sprinklers and mechanical street sweepers minimizing dust re-suspension.

Other solutions include facilitating shift to cleaner industry fuels, incentives for electric mobility uptake, stricter waste management protocols to curb dumping ground fires and pushing construction sites for better dust control.

However in majority cities, the action plans remain delayed or under-implemented owing to slow granular pollution inventory data collection, disjointed efforts across agencies, and lack of customized technological interventions.

Plus most city administrators continue relying heavily on private and personal mobility growth for urban development which hampers commensurate gains from such pollution emergency action plans.

There are also limited hard emission reduction targets for transportation, construction or industrial activities leave alone deterrent penalties regime for violations that could discipline key polluters.

Essentially while localized diagnosis and solutions have promise on paper, on ground coordination, investment, compliance issues pose roadblocks for City Action Plans to emerge from symbolic gestures to meaningful progress on clean air without fundamental governance reforms

4.3 Vehicle Emission Norms

Among the most prominent policy measures targeting air pollution mitigation is the launch of Bharat Stage VI emissions standards for vehicles in 2020, seeking to match European norms.

This regulation looks to reduce particulate matter, NOx and other greenhouse gas exhaust from on-road vehicles significantly by mandating advanced after-treatment technologies.

However, several compatibility issues confront real world conditions - poor fuel quality with high sulfur content still supplied in most cities hampers particulate filter functioning. Likewise shortage of urea for NOx control mechanisms.

Additionally, compliance testing infrastructure remains inadequate for on-road inspection of millions of vehicles for tampering or modifications bypassing after-treatment equipment. BS VI vehicle production itself faced delays.

The bigger policy blindspot lies in lenient framework for retiring old obsolete fleet running on BS III or IV standards continuing to ply unfettered lacking incentives for upgrade or phase out. Over 6 million commercial vehicles violate age limits as per analysis.

Likewise taxi and shared fleet modernization essential to impact urban air quality remains slow while non motorized or electric mobility lacks major mobility share so far. Parking policy also fails to decongest, deter private vehicle usage critical for GHG mitigation.

Essentially in the absence of synchronized multi-departmental efforts spanning stringent vehicle scrappage mandate, fuel quality supply logistics, compliance data integrity, rapid adoption policies for emerging low carbon mobility segments etc - BS VI standards alone risk remaining a ceremonial feat than substantial air pollution or carbon mitigation measure thus far.

4.4 Thermal Power Emission Rules

Coal-fired power plants are among the most notorious emitters of respirable particulates, SOx and NOx gases that choke India's regional airsheds.

Revised 2015 air pollution standards now mandate expanded use of Flue Gas Desulphurization (FGD) to cut SO2 emissions along with NOx control technologies in all existing and under construction thermal power plants.

The norms also provision zero discharge of pollutants via strict water consumption recycling norms. This signals intent on improving emissions compliance.

However, the timeline delays and waivers for financially unviable state utilities means implementation stretched till 2022 and beyond even as coal power expansion continues unabated.

There is negligible clarity on financing $15 billion capex investments needed for the FGD retrofits, causing stress on debt-ridden DISCOMs amidst renewable integration challenges. Many generators flout deadline extensions.

Coal ash ponds and mercury emissions also remain largely unregulated as thermal power lifecycle impact. And despite norms mandating online reporting of emissions monitoring data to CPCB, data transparency remains an issue.

Thus despite seemingly forward looking legislation, lack of budget commitments for thermal power green retrofits aligned to just energy transition needs, flexibility on non-compliance indicate checkered progress for the sector most critical for India meeting its climate targets and industrial air pollution burden.

4.5 Biomass Burning Ban

Paddy straw burning by farmers in North Indian states just before winter poses high risk of toxic seasonal smog each year in Delhi NCR as smoke travels.

NGT therefore ordered Haryana, Punjab etc to ensure zero crop residue incineration through monitoring networks identifying burn events via satellites and levying fines for violations under Air Act provisions.

Additionally fiscal incentives exist for supporting in-situ farm solutions like bio-gas plants, bio-CNG tractors, straw baling/ collection equipment etc that promote circular bioeconomy models without incineration.

However, limited execution capacities, reliance on village level administrators for last mile enforcement and inability of smallholder farmers to invest in alternatives given uncertainty of utilities model means over 70 million tonnes are still burned annually.

Less than 5% farmers access existing subsidies for crop residue management equipment while violations fail to instill deterrence. Cooperatives lack working capital to mainstream off-take.

Essentially lacking streamlined enforcement architecture spanning detection to penalties, the crop burning triggers deflating regional air quality annually despite blanket bans - demanding urgent policy innovation connecting economic incentives for farmers with sustainability.

4.6 Industrial Stack Monitoring

Under the Air Act, the Central Pollution Control Board (CPCB) in last few years expanded continuous emissions monitoring systems to over 7000 sites across highly polluting industries like steel, cement, textiles, chemicals etc.

This mandates large facilities to install automated equipment analyzing and reporting load of particulate matter, SOx, NOx spewed out 24x7 to CPCB for checks on pollution thresholds.

However, discrepancies exist in transparency over emissions inventory publication, calibration certifications and verification protocols for accuracy of monitoring equipment installed by plants themselves lacking independent oversight.

Pollutant concentration permissible limits also require further tightening while penalty regime remains lenient lacking deterrent fines on persistent violators leave aside temporary shuttering powers to regulators unlike soln arbitration etc

Essentially while stack monitoring and digitization of emissions compliance signals right intent, lack of integrity in data gathering protocols and lax enforcements frameworks diminish impact currently from this flagship program to discipline India's industrial air pollution load - demanding significant reforms.

4.7 Judiciary Interventions

In absence of commensurate executive action, India's judiciaryespecially the Supreme Court and National Green Tribunal has had to repeatedly step in to pull up both central and state agencies on tardy implementation around air quality management.

Be it ensuring stricter timelines for BS VI vehicle emission norms adoption or direct accountability for thermal power plants persisting with missing FGD equipment, the courts have passed significant directions for compliance.

Likewise recent ruling banning petcoke use by industries, ordering civic bodies to distribute anti-pollution masks to labor communities during severe episodes acknowledges health impacts.

NGT also passed directives for responsible garbage disposal by municipal bodies after recurring incidents of toxic dump yard fires exacerbating seasonal pollution in cities like Delhi.

Courts also enforce bans around riskprone activities like open waste burning, firecrackers etc against transient electoral pressures.

Yet overarching weaknesses in environmental regulation architecture often requires repeat judicial interventions treating symptoms rather than system strengthening towards sustainable industrialization and energy security policies protecting air quality as public health imperative beyond mere ambient counts

* * *

CHAPTER 5: THE ROAD AHEAD FOR CITIES, TOWNS & RURAL AREAS

5.1 Overview of Policy Intervention Areas

Transportation

Goals: 100% new vehicles sales to be electric by 2030, complete phase out of diesel vehicles by 2040

Interventions:

Metros:

- Rail network expansion target to be increased from 500km per city to 1000km per city covering wider city clusters
- Develop 25 high capacity metro lines (similar to Delhi Airport Express Line) connecting airports and satellite townships
- Electric feeder vehicles should cover 50% of first/last

mile rides through permits and purchase incentives

- Congestion charges to be dynamically linked to real-time traffic and pollution levels

Smaller Cities:

- Increase dedicated BRTS network target to 150 km per city with bus frequencies under 5 minutes during peak hours
- Cycling infrastructure to cover 50% of arterial roads with segregated tracks protecting safety
- Promote electric 2 and 3-wheelers through preferential registration and exemption from road taxes

Rural:

- Provide 50% capital cost subsidies for purchase of electric vehicles for rural usage like tractors and shared mobility vehicles
- Install modular bioCNG plants across villages to convert agricultural waste to clean cooking gas
- Subsidize operation costs of rural electric mobility entrepreneurs for 5 years through viability gap funding

Case Studies:

- China's Rural Biogas Program reached 50 million rural households with clean gas
- Delhi Metro Rail success in expanding public transportation ridership 5 fold
- EV incentives in Norway and California driving mainstream electric adoption

Budget Needed:

- Updated budget requirement to $50 billion over 10 years
- Allocate $25 billion for metros, $15 billion for smaller

cities distribution across states, $10 billion for rural clean transportation promotions

Power Generation

Goals: 65% renewables in energy mix by 2030, shut down old thermal plants below critical size

Interventions:

Large Scale Renewables

- Solar: Add 100 GW utility scale solar parks through accelerated tendering and acquisition @ $1 million per MW

- Wind: Add 50 GW onshore and 10 GW offshore wind energy generation capacity @ $2 million per MW

- Transmission Corridors: Expand national grid transmission network by 50% for renewable energy evacuation

Distributed Solar

- Rooftop Solar: Mandate and subsidize rooftop capacity for 50% commercial and 30% industrial power need

- Residential Solar: Provide capital subsidies covering 30% system costs for 20 million households

Biomass Power

- Agricultural Waste: Incentivize farmers to aggregate and supply crop residue to biomethane plants through MSP support

- CBG Plants: Setup 5000 compact bioCNG plants through hybrid annuity model

Case Studies:

- Texas and Iowa's wind power growth through proactive policies
- Bangladesh's success with rooftop solar integration
- Sweden bioCNG production meeting 50% vehicle fuel needs

Updated Budget Needed:

- Total $500 billion over 10 years
- Breakup:
    - $350 billion for large scale solar, wind and transmission
    - $100 billion for rooftop solar subsidies
    - $50 billion for biomass reuse supply chain development

Industry

Goals: 50% reduction target for air pollutants from factories, industrial clusters by 2030

Interventions:

Strict Emission & Efficiency Norms

- Tighten PM, NOx, SOx norms by 50% over 5 years for highly polluting sectors like steel, cement, chemicals
- Mandate energy efficiency benchmarks aligned with global best practice for SMEs

Technology Upgradation Subsidies

- Provide incentive packages covering 30% of technology capital costs for MSMEs
- Setup industry-specific clean tech expertise centers for adoption hand-holding

Cluster Relocation Scheme

- Identify and close select urban industrial clusters contradicting master plans
- Offer 50% rental support for relocation to special processing zones in 2 years

Case Studies:

- South Korea's Environment Conservation Fund to drive SME transformation
- China's industrial cluster shutdowns and upgrades lowering Beijing pollution
- Gujarat's special textile park boosting efficiency

Updated Budget Needed:

- Total $150 billion over 10 years
- Breakup:
    - $50 billion for technology migration subsidies
    - $75 billion for industrial cluster relocation fund
    - $25 billion for administration and monitoring mechanisms

Waste Management

Goals: Achieve essential waste collection services for all towns/ cities by 2025, 100% waste segregation and 80% recycling rates for major cities by 2030

Interventions:

Door-to-Door Collection

- Mandate source segregation and daily waste pickup services across households, shops, offices in urban areas through municipal laws
- Daily collection needed from vegetable markets, meat shops, restaurants managing higher organic waste
- Deploy fleet of e-carts for separate wet and dry waste equipped with lids, lined bins to prevent spillage
- App-based pickup scheduling and route optimization to plan demand-driven trips reducing fuel costs
- RFID tagging of household and shop bins for activity logging integrated with user charges payments
- Metric-based incentives for zone-level waste collection supervisors linked to adoption rates
- Allow informal waste workers integration into collection units after required training

Service Level Guidelines:

- Minimum daily pickup in high-density areas, alternate day collection in peripheral zones
- Maximum 1 km distance between households and

nearest bin enclosures

- Waste bins standardization for capacity, colors indicating waste types

Supporting Infrastructure:

- Material recovery facility in each zone for sorting waste post collection, pre-processing

- decentralized composting or biomethanation plants to locally process biodegradable portion

- Garbage transfer stations with compactors to aggregate and transport waste to regional landfills

Decentralized Processing

Regional Waste-to-Energy Plants

- Setup plants to process 500+ tons per day of municipal waste through PPP models

- RDF extraction technology to produce fuel pellets for co-processing in cement kilns, coal plants

- Biomethane production through anaerobic digestion for injections into gas pipeline networks

- Environmental standards compliance for emissions, effluents discharge enforced strictly

Fiscal Incentives for Localized Units

- 30-50% capital cost subsidies for micro composting and plastics recycling ventures

- Generous land allocation, property tax waivers for decentralized plants

- Soft loans and credit guarantees for new entrepreneurs in waste processing domain

Supporting Infrastructure Requirements

- Segregated waste supply chain from source to regional plants via transfer stations
- Logistics ecosystem providing connectivity to waste-derivative off takers
- Testing labs and incubation centers to promote indigenous recycling innovations

Implementation Strategies

- Cluster based project allocations to drive economies of scale
- Output based rewards upon achieving waste diversion goals and adoption targets

Awareness Campaigns

Mass Media Drives

- Television and radio campaigns focused on source segregation starring celebrity influencers
- Localize content highlighting waste issues to emotionally connect target communities
- Partner with religious congregations and community centers as messaging platforms

Waste Management in Academic Curriculum

- Introduce customized curriculum for school students focused on segregation, recycling, composting
- Make certification courses mandatory for college students across disciplines
- Launch innovation challenges and field projects linking waste hierarchy concepts to solutions

Community Mobilization

- Leverage youth groups, RWAs, NGOs for door-to-door awareness activities
- Conduct street plays and activation drives during festivals incorporating waste messaging
- Display signages near dumping hotspots creatively capturing essence of circular economy

Tracking Effectiveness

- Commission annual surveys to measure awareness levels and behavior shifts
- Technology interventions like RFID tags, sensors to map actual adoption rates across neighborhood

Global Best Practices

Swiss Cities Waste Management

- High waste taxes enforced by weight and volume making dumping expensive
- Mandated recycling discipline ingrained over 30 years achieving 80-90% rates
- Robust logistics for segregated municipal waste collection through user charges
- Adoption driven by social consciousness instead of penalties alone

Key Enablers:

- Decentralized processing infrastructure scaled ward by ward
- Consistent policy direction aligning taxes to circular economy goals

- Transparent monitoring of waste footprint by households

Swedish Waste-to-Energy Model

- Pioneers in extracting energy from waste since 1970s given lack of fossil fuels
- 52 specialized waste-to-energy plants countrywide producing heat and electricity
- Enabled by carbon and landfill taxes incentivizing capital investment
- Compliance with strict environmental standards for residual ash disposal

Adoption Considerations for India:

- Align user charges, pollution taxes to principles of circular economy
- Build decentralized infrastructure through cluster based investments
- Drive technology innovations in waste valorization suiting local context
- Robust monitoring mechanism providing transparency on adoption

Updated Budget: $30 billion

Service Delivery Infrastructure ($10 billion)

- $5 billion for door-to-door collection fleet across urban and rural areas
- $3 billion allocated towards material recovery facilities and transfer stations
- $2 billion for centralized waste processing plants

(waste-to-energy, composting etc)

Fiscal Incentives ($5 billion)

- $2 billion capital subsidies for micro scale decentralized processing units
- $2 billion interest subsidies on loans for waste management enterprises
- $1 billion tax incentives and incentives linked to waste diversion goals

Awareness Drives ($1 billion)

- $500 million for multimedia content creation and dissemination
- $300 million towards mobilization drives led by NGOs, youth groups
- $200 million allocated for school and college curriculum development

Governance & Monitoring ($3 billion)

- $2 billion for command centers, sensor networks, RFID infrastructure
- $1 billion for oversight bodies, certifications, annual surveys

Construction & Road Dust

Goals:

- Enforce updated construction guidelines meeting WHO air quality standards across cities by 2025
- Mandatory paving of road shoulders on national and state highways by 2027

Key Interventions:

Construction Sites Emission Control

- Special site management guidelines covering excavation, carriage, concreting activities
- Green hydrogen deployment for diesel generator replacement at large project sites
- Strict dust pollution norms implemented through special enforcement agencies

Minimizing Road Dust Resuspension

- Expand tree coverage along major traffic corridors to provide air purification cover
- Paving of road shoulders wherever feasible to limit loose soil patches prone to dust
- Vacuum-based cleaning mechanisms for heavy traffic zones to capture fine particles

Global Best Practices

- Japan's Next Generation Construction program sets high standards through certification
- Germany's air treatment roads with catalyst coated paving to breakdown NOx gases

Updated Budget: $15 billion

- $5 billion for mechanized construction equipment upgrades
- $3 billion for roadside greening drives and paving
- $2 billion for specialized site/street cleaning machinery

Agricultural Burning

Goals: Complete elimination of crop residue open burning by 2027

Interventions:

Demand Side Measures

- Setup decentralized compact bio-CNG plants and biomass pellets production units
- Enable farmer collectives to aggregate and supply crop residue to decentralized plants
- Provide market development support for crop waste derived energy products

Supply Side Measures

- Promote crop diversification away from paddy to less residue-intensive crops
- Setup farm machinery banks offering zero tillage, shredding equipment use on pay-per-use basis

Global Best Practices

- China's region-specific crop residue reuse roadmaps with decentralized capacity building
- Canada's agricultural equipment purchase subsidies increasing adoption of conservational techniques

Updated Budget: $20 billion

- $10 billion for setting up biomass reuse supply chain infrastructure
- $5 billion for crop diversification and equipment promotion schemes
- $5 billion for administration, monitoring and awareness drives

Blueprint for Metros

Special Policy Measures

- Transport: Vehicle restriction rules, congestion charges, electric vehicles promotion
- Construction: Site management guidelines, green building material incentives
- Waste: Decentralized processing infrastructure, incineration plants

Best Practices Delhi NCR:

- Expanded metro network with feeder systems
- Graded vehicle restriction rules under critical pollution episodes
- Increased biomethane production through waste processing

Mumbai:

- Robust inland waterways-based freight transport reducing trucks
- Rooftop solar power adoption through net metering incentives
- Mangrove afforestation driving carbon sequestration

Case Studies on Highly Polluted Mega Cities Beijing, China

- Temporary shut down of factories, demolition of polluting clusters
- Shift of non-essential industry to neighboring satellite cities
- Priority vehicles lanes introduced promoting public transport

Mexico City, Mexico

- Successful implementation of vehicle restriction rules over 20 years
- Integration of cycling infrastructure across mobility planning
- Significant waste recycling rates driven by economic incentives

Blueprint for Smaller Towns & Cities

Tailored Policies

- Cleaner vehicles and fuels: Incentives for CNG, EV adoption suited for shorter distances
- Decentralized renewables: Rooftop solar mandates for commercial buildings, off-grid solutions
- Cluster-based approach: Developing economic zones with integrated waste and energy infrastructure

Learnings from Indian Towns Indore:

- High-impact municipal transformation within limited budgets
- Door-to-door waste collection integrating rag-pickers
- Increased biogas generation from waste

Panaji:

- Promoting walking and cycling through public bicycle sharing initiative
- Task forces setup to drive adoption of green buildings
- Multi-modal mobility planning optimizing road usage

Global Small Town Best Practices Freiburg, Germany:

- Car-free urban village design principles enabling non-motorized transit
- District level heating and cooling infrastructure powered by renewables
- High waste recycling rates through household discipline.

Blueprint for Rural Areas

Electric Vehicles Promotion

- 50% capital subsidies on purchase of electric agriculture equipment like tractors, water pumps
- Incentives for electric auto-rickshaws as shared mobility model serving clusters of villages
- Preferential financing schemes through state cooperative banks

Modular BioCNG Plants

- Standardized compact system design enabling distributed deployment with ~100 ton input
- Capability to handle heterogeneous agri-waste from crop residues to dairy manure
- Output options - piped biogas for community kitchens or CBG for vehicles

Operational Subsidies

- Viability gap funding for electric vehicle leasing entrepreneurs in villages
- Cover fixed costs like battery replacements, electricity connections etc
- Tied to service level conditions like uptime, customer reach over 5 years

Support Infrastructure

- Renewables-driven EV charging hubs at panchayat offices
- Skill training programs for youth to operate bioCNG plants, EV fleet maintenance
- Progress monitoring against continues energy access and livelihood creation goals

National & Sub-National Governance Models

1. Integrated Central Command Center

- Converged structure combining CPCB, BEE, Ministry wings monitoring air quality programs
- Digital platform integrating emissions data, policy notifications, complaints management
- Dashboards providing national, state and city level tracking against reduction targets

2. State Level Command Centers

- Convergence of SPCBs, Urban Development Authorities, Renewable Energy Agencies
- City specific air quality management plan development, implementation and monitoring
- Bottom-up data aggregation from municipal bodies on adoption of initiatives

3. Urban Local Bodies Coordination

- Ward committees engagement in localized planning and

community awareness

- Unified information system around emissions inventory, ambient monitoring and reporting
- Cross functional collaboration on key issues - transport, waste management, green spaces

National Clean Air Finance Corporation

- Special funding vehicle under Central Government to drive major state and city-level programs
- Budget allocation combining government contribution, multi-lateral assistance, market borrowing

Cooperative Federalism

- Enabling framework recognizing local context allowing customized policy approaches
- Central policies acting as guiding principles around ambient air quality benchmarks
- Knowledge hub for global best practice sharing, capacity building and technological expertise

Key Takeaways for Governance Blueprint

- Converged command framework cutting across institutional silos
- Cohesive ambient monitoring, emissions accounting and reporting protocols
- Cooperative model aligning local actions to national policy direction
- Dedicated financing vehicle de-risking public and private investments

National Clean Air Fund

- Expand scope to fund major state and city level programs on air quality management

- Corpus to be raised from budget allocation, pollution taxes, multi-lateral assistance
- Governed by a board chaired by the Environment Minister with state representations
- Fund allocation towards capital investments and incentive programs

Focus Investment Areas:

- Scaling renewable energy and cleantech projects
- Retrofits, upgrades and maintenance in industrial sectors
- Expansion of public transportation and EV ecosystem
- Municipal waste processing infrastructure
- Monitoring technology deployment

State-Level Clean Air Financing Corporations

- State level corporations to drive context specific clean air investments
- Mandate to design financial instruments to bridge viability gap in projects
- Budgets from respective state contributions, market borrowings, bonds
- Provide variety of instruments - equity, debt, mezzanine capital, guarantees etc.

Focus Initiatives:

- Support to MSMEs for replacing legacy pollution equipment
- First loss guarantees for urban waste processing PPP projects
- Capital subsidies for renewable energy micro and mini grid systems

- Soft loans for electric vehicles promotion across user segments

Critical Success Factors

- Committed leadership and multisector partnerships
- Performance management frameworks to track progress
- Leveraging monitoring technologies like sensors and satellite data

Committed Leadership

- Central empowered committee constituted to drive air quality management agenda
- Headed by Principal Scientific Advisor with members from environment, power, transport, industry, agriculture ministries
- Set policy direction, approves state action plans, reviews annual progress

Robust Capacity Building

- Structured training curriculum for personnel across municipal, transport, PCBs, infrastructure departments
- Central program in collaboration with international agencies like UNDP, WHO, World Bank
- Tailored capacity building targeting execution roles - program managers, inspectors, ops engineers
- Training inventory and outcome monitoring against

performance efficiency metrics

Extensive Public Awareness

- Partnerships with media houses for consistent messaging around air quality issues

- Utilize diverse platforms - TV, radio, print, social media for localized context

- Community activation drives lead by prominent citizen groups and NGOs

- Sustained engagement with public designed as movement rather than one-off campaign

The focus is on streamlining governance machinery while enabling execution capabilities and public momentum to drive policies aimed at impactful and tangible reduction in emissions across key sectors

Conclusion & Key Takeaways

Integrated Framework

- Holistic blueprint binding intervention areas into common emission reduction vision
- Interlinkages across sectors established - transport electrification feeding renewable expansion, waste processing supplying biofuels
- Unified guidelines for governing bodies interaction across focus areas and statkeholders

Critical Success Factors

- Committed leadership via empowered committee driving relentless execution
- Robust information architecture enabling diagnostics andCorrective measures
- Institutional capabilities built through targeted capacity enhancement

Vision for Clean Air Future

- Breathable air quality achieved across urban and rural regions by 2030
- Economic growth rebalanced aligning pollution impacts
- Production and consumption choices steered by ecological conscience
- Quality of life uplifted with sustainable resource utilization
- India emerging as model for developing countries to emulate

The integrated framework transforms dispersed efforts into

mass movement leveraging interlinkages across sectors, governance machinery, technologies and behavioral change - ultimately targeting tangible health and climate impact

* * *

CHAPTER 6: BUDGETS AND INVESTMENTS REQUIRED

6.1 budget requirement

Transportation: $50 billion

- Metros expansion: $25 billion
- EVs incentives: $10 billion
- Rural access programs: $15 billion

Power Generation: $500 billion

- Solar parks: $200 billion
- Wind power: $150 billion
- Rooftop solar subsidies: $100 billion
- Transmission revamp: $50 billion

Industry: $150 billion

- Technology migration subsidies: $50 billion
- Cluster relocation fund: $75 billion
- Governance & monitoring: $25 billion

Waste Management: $30 billion

- Collection infrastructure: $10 billion
- Fiscal incentives: $5 billion
- Awareness drives: $1 billion
- Governance & monitoring: $3 billion

Construction & Road Dust: $15 billion

- Construction equipment upgrade: $5 billion
- Roadside vegetation drives: $3 billion
- Monitoring & governance: $2 billion

Agricultural Burning: $20 billion

- Biomass supply infrastructure: $10 billion
- Crop diversification schemes: $5 billion
- Administration & awareness: $5 billion

Total Envelope: $800 billion

- Split over 5-7 year horizon
- Front loaded allocation to power, industry, transport to enable high abatement

6.2 Financing Avenues

Government Funding:

- Additional budget allocation of 0.5% of GDP per year towards clean air programs
- Phase out fossil fuel subsidies and redirect funds to renewable energy and EV ecosystem

Market-based Instruments:

- Expand carbon trading mechanisms to wider industrial sectors
- Impose higher taxes on polluting fuels like coal and diesel
- Congestion charges, parking levies in urban areas funding public transport

Multilateral Assistance

- Global climate funds offering soft loans and grants prioritizing air pollution projects
- Support from agencies like ADB, World Bank towards rooftop solar, waste management

Innovative Bonds:

- Municipal bonds supporting electric buses procurement backed by user fee collection
- Dedicated clean air bonds from government backed by green cess allocation

Blended Capital:

- Viability gap funding pooled from public and private sources
- Anchor investors committing capital if execution

benchmarks met over time

The combination of budgets, market-linked instruments, financial engineering solutions and global capital flows can meet the sizeable investment requirement in sustainable manner.

6.3 Structuring National Clean Air Fund

Objectives

- Mobilize sizeable pool of capital exclusively towards air pollution control initiatives
- Enable centralized governance on fund allocation aligned to policy priorities

Sources of Funds

- Initial corpus grant allocation over 5 years in Union Budget
- Expanding pool through special clean air cess on polluting fuels
- Market borrowings against future cess allocation

Governance Framework

- Governing council chaired by Finance Minister including stakeholder ministry representatives
- Independent investment evaluation committee recommending allocation plan
- Output and outcome-based monitoring process

Focus Application Areas

- Subsidies supporting adoption of electric vehicles and charging infrastructure
- Capital investment towards renewable energy parks for clean power access
- Support to municipal bodies for waste processing and recycling infrastructure
- Grants for industrial MSMEs to install emissions control equipment

The unified structure allows consolidated planning, governance and impact tracking on key result areas to drive tangible reduction in emissions intensity

6.4 Supplementary Revenue Streams

1. Pollution Penalties

- 25-100% hike in non-compliance fines imposed by pollution control boards
- Enable deterrence towards continuous offense by industrial units
- Earmark incremental penalty revenue for related infrastructure aids

2. Congestion Charges & Levies

- Dynamic congestion fees in cities funding electric vehicles promotion
- Parking charges hikes channelized to sidewalks/cycling infrastructure
- Land value capture financing models around transit upgrades

3. Betterment Levies

- Infrastructure upgrades enabling social and environmental benefits
- Value created recovered partially by levying beneficiary communities
- Illustration: Sewage connectivity project funded by one-time charges

4. Voluntary Carbon Offsets

- Expand eligible project categories under carbon markets
- Credits purchase by corporates and individuals
- Climate action themed CSR, crowdfunding campaigns

5. Cooperative Financing Models

- Community-shared solar power infra funded by interest-bearing deposits

- Local farmer entrepreneur networks running decentralized bio-CNG plants

This expands avenues beyond traditional budget routes and borrowing for self-sustaining project funding structures aligned to circular economy principles

3-year action plan with phasing of budget utilization and links to air quality improvement milestones:

Year 1

- Budget Utilization: $200 billion

- Key Result Areas:
    - 50% target achievement:
        - Renewable energy generation capacity
        - Electric vehicles sales share
        - Municipal waste processing infrastructure
    - 25% target achievement:
        - Industrial emissions reduction
        - Construction guidelines enforcement

- Air Quality Milestones:
    - 10-15% reduction target in annual average PM2.5, PM10 levels

Year 2

- Budget Utilization: $250 billion

- Key Result Areas:
    - 100% target achievement:
        - Renewable capacity addition
        - Municipal waste processing coverage
    - 50% target achievement:
        - EV sales share
        - Industrial emissions reduction

- Air Quality Milestones:
    - 15-20% reduction in peak pollution episode intensity

Year 3:

- Budget Utilization: $150 billion
- Key Result Areas:
    - 100% target achievement:
        - EV sales share
        - Construction norms enforcement
    - 75% target achievement:
        - Industrial emissions reduction
- Air Quality Milestones:
    - 20-25% reduction in number of non-compliant days
    - 10-15% reduction in annual average pollution levels

The phasing allows front-loading infrastructure development in renewable energy, storage solutions, electric mobility and waste management for tangible pollution cuts.

* * *

CHAPTER 7: SOCIETAL ADVOCACY AND ACTIVISM

7.1 Grassroots Activism Driving Change

Case Study 1: Protests Against Construction Impacting Ecology in Mumbai

Background:

- Infrastructure projects planned affecting forestland and wetlands in Mumbai

- Worli-Bandra Sea Link requiring reclamation impacting coastal terrain

Public Reaction:

- Large scale mobilization by citizen groups under umbrella of "Save Mumbai's Environment"

- Peaceful protests, human chains capturing media attention

Outcomes:

- Forced authorities to conduct public consultation

addressing concerns

- Projects tweaked to minimize ecological impact through alternative alignment
- Compensatory afforestation mandate around other infrastructure sites

Key Takeaways:

- Coordinated activism creates visibility compelling policy response
- Arguments rooted in scientific data makes movement more credible
- Sustained civic participation ensures construction norms enforcement

Similar mass movements were instrumental across India's metro cities forcing realignments of transport corridors like elevated highways reducing direct impact on tree cover and habitat fragmentation. This highlights the ability of inclusive participation based on rational arguments to positively influence infrastructure development priorities.

Case Study 2: Public Interest Litigation Driving Air Pollution Control Reforms in Delhi

Background:

- Delhi witnessing severe air quality decline over past decades
- Multiple policy announcements by governments without rigorous enforcement on ground

Litigation Facts:

- Civil society representatives filed public interest litigations since early 2000s
- Key agenda - vehicular emission control, fuel quality improvement, construction norms

Court Orders & Outcomes:

- Supreme Court and NGT judgments between 2001-2015 imposed gradually tighter emissions standards
- Forced authorities to strictly comply on restricting plying of old commercial diesel vehicles
- Mandated construction site management guidelines including dust mitigation measures

On-Ground Impact:

- Litigation pressure expedited more decisive policy action attribution
- Old diesel vehicles phase out timeline advanced by over 5 years through court order
- Pollution norms enforcement prioritized by setting up monitoring committee

Key Takeaways:

- Petitions make government legally accountable to act as per constitutional right to clean air

- Petitioners presentation of technical evidence on pollution sources played vital role

- Sustained involvement by original filers in monitoring implementation ensures continuity

Case Study 3: Right to Breathe Movement - India

Campaign Overview:

- Launched in 2019 by climate activist groups in major cities

- Demand stronger state and national action towards clean air

- Mass citizen engagement through festivals, human chains, awareness drives

Key Engagement Avenues:

- Art Installations: Interactive pollution murals, street art

- Digital activism: Creative hashtags, tweet-a-thons

- Influencer partnerships: Sport stars, actors amplification

Achievement Highlights:

- Expanded National Clean Air Program to 100+ cities

- Boosted budget allocations on monitoring infrastructure

- Renewed commitments from state leaders on emission goals

Takeaways:

- Inclusive campaigns sustain public interest and momentum

- Multichannel outreach maximizes reach and impact

- Outcome linkage to firm policy commitments elevates credibility

Applicability for Replication:

- Pollution visibility drives higher concern converting

into impact

- Strong research backing quantifying issues adds credibility
- Celebrity influencers involvement brings mass appeal

Attributes Of Impactful Activism

Persistent and Committed Leadership:

- Sustained effort spanning years instead of short bursts
- Leaders overcoming frustrations using emotional resilience
- Institutionalization allowing transition across multiple generations of activists

Inclusive and Participative Approach:

- Mainstreaming environmentalism across all sections of society
- Ensuring representation from marginalized communities facing disproportionate pollution impacts
- Mobilizing public participation through creative engagement models

Thoughtful and Evidence-Based Demands

- Clear articulation of demands backed by rigorous research evidence
- Technically sound pollution analysis and policy alternatives formulation
- Legal standing reinforced by presenting constitutional rights basis

Importance of Sound Understanding

- Problem quantification through data indicators tracking

issues over time

- Evidence enhancing credibility compelling authorities to respond

Creative Communication for Inspiration

- Impactful photography building visual imagery
- Narrative storytelling around personal impactful experiences
- Art, music, plays conveying message through emotion

7.2 Avenues for Mass Action

Leveraging Art Forms

- Street art, wall graffiti for pollution awareness
- Street plays dramatizing impact of air toxins performed at public squares
- Billboards hacking with green messages through printed overlays

Technology Platforms

- Geo-tagged reporting apps on pollution complaints, tree cutting incidents
- Virtual coordination allowing distributed volunteers participation
- Gamification elements increasing retention via rewards

Grassroots Innovation Challenges

- Prizes for decentralized waste and water innovations by local communities
- Maker spaces access provided for prototype design across schools, universities

- Solutions incubated further by public agencies

Crowdfunding Models

- Online fundraising for community led air quality interventions
- Matching grants by local representatives and corporates
- Progress documentation building credibility for additional grants

Key Recommendations

Global Mindset + Local Action

- Community level problem diagnosis and priorities alignment
- Globally proven solution implementation customized for local context

Corporate Partnerships

- Employee volunteering supporting environmental non-profits
- Pro-bono consulting assistance on strategy, technology adoption
- Co-branded D2C product lines funding cause promotions

7.3 Sustaining Momentum with the Young Generation

Promoting Sustainability-Focused Social Entrepreneurship

- Incubation programs at universities targeting student entrepreneurs with environment-related solutions
- Access to fab-labs for prototyping assistance with pollution control devices or precision agriculture
- Accelerators supported by industry associations and CSR funds to refine products to market readiness

Competitions & Events

- National level challenges for student innovators solving local pollution issues
- Hackathons focused on clean technologies co-hosted by start-up networks
- Conferences as networking platforms connecting green entrepreneurs to funding avenues

Enabling Policies

- Relaxed procurement norms for piloting innovations from new ventures
- Bid exemptions and fast-tracked land access for setting up pilot projects
- Environmental clearances assistance through dedicated facilitation desks

Financing Avenues

- Clean air themed venture capital funds with alumni HNI participation
- Debt instruments by impact investors – convertible notes, revenue-based financing
- Outcome-based grants releasing tranches upon achieving adoption milestones

This comprehensive entrepreneurial ecosystem design leverages the dynamism of youth to deliver market-driven, scalable solutions tailored for pollution challenges in Indian cities while boosting sustainability-focused start-up growth.

Building Interdisciplinary Academic Models

Course Structuring

- Core curriculum integration - air quality sciences mandatory for engineers and architects
- Joint electives pairing technology and social sciences students for collaborative projects

Experiential Learning

- Tinkering labs for designing market-relevant innovations addressing local pollution issues
- Student internships at urban governance bodies, cleantech startups and environmental NGOs

Extracurricular Programing

- Sustainability bootcamps focused on frugal innovations for pollution control
- Professional student chapters promoting cross-faculty interaction and alignment

Joint Research Avenues

- Interdisciplinary centers focused on sustainability projects pairing science, engineering and policy researchers
- Conferences, seminar series and panels encouraging diverse expertise conversations

Intended Outcomes

- Holistic framing of sustainability challenges spanning science, technology and social realms

- Enhanced solution orientation leveraging strong analytical rigor and human-centric mindfulness
- Tight researcher-practitioner linkages identifying real problems requiring scholarly investigation

Communication Leveraging Youth Culture Avenues:

Leveraging Youth Culture Avenues

Sports Integration

- Sponsoring pollution awareness cycles, runs, marathons with participation certificates
- Captive engagement at colleges festivals with activites like clean air themed wall arts
- Sport stars as campaign ambassadors promoting tree plantation pledges

Music and Performing Arts

- Original pro-environment songs compositions competitions at the school level
- Rap battles with lyrics focused on renewable energy promotion in rural areas
- Flash mobs organized by youth groups highlighting waste management

Visual Arts

- Inter-school competitions for drawings, sketches on air pollution harms
- DIY workshops building small-scale purifying plants, vertical gardens for homes
- Exhibitions showcasing creativity in utilizing recycled materials for arts

Impact Potential

- Mass appeal tapping into interests like sports, music, creativity and activism
- Peer influence and aspiration value driving large scale engagement
- Relatability and retention of messaging heightened

This blends pro-sustainability values promotion with youth popular culture allowing sticky communication that travels faster across school and college networks to maximize reach and recall.

* * *

CHAPTER 8: PARTNERSHIPS FOR CHANGE

8.1 Role of Citizens

A. Embracing Clean Lifestyle Choices

Sustainable Transportation Choices:

- Walking, cycling prioritized for intra-city commutes under 5 km

- Public transport usage normalized for longer distances through improved service quality

- Shared mobility models encouraged over personal vehicle ownership for optimized utilization

- Shift to electric vehicles for unavoidable personal transport needs in a staggered manner

Energy Efficiency Adoption:

- Transitioning to LED lighting fixtures phasing out

inefficient bulbs across households

- Upgrading to 5-star rated electrical appliances, cooling units during replacement cycles
- Adoption of smart energy management technologies syncing with decentralized solar generation
- Community outreach focused on switching off lights and appliances when not required

Sustainable Consumption Habits:

- Practice of 'Reduce, Reuse and Recycle' instilled through awareness campaigns and school curriculum
- Promoting up-cycled, recycled products adoption through eco-labelling incentives
- Incentives encouraging voluntary moderation of chemical-based personal care and sanitary products usage

Dietary Shifts for Lower Emissions:

- Gradual decrease in meat proteins, dairy products consumption in alignment with global guidelines
- Promotion of plant-based protein sources through farmers markets and special procurement incentives
- Dietary guidelines highlighting emissions intensity of foods for conscious consumption

Fundamental realignments in consumption patterns can significantly moderate India's ecological footprint while improving environmental quality, public health and equitable resource utilization

B. Volunteering And Awareness Building

Community Clean-Up Drives

- Periodically organizing neighborhood litter pick-up campaigns in public spaces
- Involve local youth groups, residential associations in driving participation
- Structured clean-up competitions introducing gamification elements

Plantation Drives

- Organizing tree sapling plantation events celebrating environment days
- Adopting parks, open areas for developing urban forests cover
- Volunteer coordination for post-plantation maintenance and watering

Conscious Living Promotion

- Awareness sessions highlighting waste segregation practices
- Sharing home composting techniques, setup guidance for community adoption
- Demonstrating usage of products made from recycled materials

Outreach through Networks

- Deploying volunteers for door-to-door awareness building across neighborhoods
- Engagement through resident welfare associations, community centers
- Leveraging as champions for grassroots communication campaigns

This local mobilization strengthens shared ownership on environmental sustainability mission while enabling micro-scale changes in consumption and waste habits that collectively manifest as major impact over time.

Participating in Governance

Municipal Involvement:

- Attending municipal council meetings to voice concerns on sanitation, waste management
- Pressing for transparency by demanding access to project documents, budgets, air quality data
- Demanding accountability towards commitments on service delivery benchmarks

Infrastructure Feedback:

- Staying vigilant of upcoming infrastructure projects in local area
- Submitting feedback during public consultation on environmental impact assessments
- Organizing community groups to press for re-alignment, mitigation measures adoption

Clean Air Action Plans:

- Engaging with city authorities on formulation of sector-wise pollution reduction strategies
- Contributing localized insights into root causes and prioritization of key intervention areas
- Monitoring implementation through NGO collaborations and independent audits

This active participation strengthens environmental governance by making public bodies more responsive. It fosters inclusion of citizens' concerns into policy formulation and enforcement, enhancing ownership.

Enablers:

- Statutory provisions for public consultation and

disclosure in development projects

- Forums for civil society representation in advisory capacities to urban local bodies

- Dedicated social audits of civic programs aided by civil society groups and volunteers

Consistent engagement levels the accountability playing field by compelling public agencies to factor in health and environmental priorities into policy choices and program design.

Financial Support for Initiatives

Community-led Pollution Control Ideas

- Crowdsourced microfinancing for neighbourhood composting facilities, tree plantation drives
- Crowdfunding and community pooling to setup air purification systems in schools, hospitals
- Fiscal participation models like community bonds for installing renewable energy infrastructure

Environmental Legal Support

- Contributing to fundraising campaigns by public interest litigators fighting pollution cases
- Citizen-funded legal research for identifying policy gaps requiring course correction
- Pro-bono lawyers volunteering time for drafting court petitions and proceedings

Cleantech Social Entrepreneurship

- Crowd-investing in innovative pollution control ventures, prototypes and pilot projects
- Collective community procurement driving volumes for decentralized solutions adoption
- Venture philanthropy providing seed funding for earlystage clean technology startups

This collective mobilization of financial resources democratizes the innovation ecosystem. It enhances affordability and access to decentralized solutions while furthering environmental causes.

Enablers:

- Regulatory clarity allowing crowdfunding platforms to focus on cause-specific campaigns

- Tax incentives to catalyze seed-stage impact investing into sustainability-oriented ventures

- Policies simplifying public procurement procedures to pilot innovative community solutions

8.2 Corporate Contributions

As key drivers of economic growth, the business sector has a vital role in India's transition to a sustainable, low-emissions development trajectory. Corporate entities must leverage their engineering capabilities, operational capacity and financial resources to embed environmental priorities across value chains. Innovative solutions stemming from private sector R&D, conscious business leadership, and policy advocacy can catalyze systemic impact in conjunction with governmental initiatives.

I. Technology Innovation and CleanTech Promotion

The private sector must prioritise green research and development to deliver technological breakthroughs addressing emissions challenges. Besides internal innovation pipelines, corporations should extend support to cleantech startups through incubation assistance, venture investments and market access partnerships.

Focus Areas

- Electric mobility ecosystem - Batteries, charging infrastructure, fleet services

- Renewables and storage technologies - Offshore wind, solid-state batteries

- Industrial pollutants control - Sensors, catalysts, process innovation

Corporate Cleantech Collaboration Models

- Venture capital funds for early-stage sustainability

ventures

- Research grants to academia and labs for emissions reduction projects

- Joint development agreements facilitating technology licensing and commercialization

- Supplier diversity programs engaging with minority-founded green businesses

Case Study: General Electric's EcomagineNation Initiative Through over $200 million in support to institutions, startups, individuals and communities, GE accelerates adoption of cleantech solutions globally. Focus areas range from renewable energy and grid technology to energy efficient appliances.

II. Advocacy and Policy Influence

Beyond technology pathways, private sector facilitation is vital in shaping frameworks conducive for transformative change. Corporations providing technical evidence for policies while demonstrating model leadership inspires broader adoption and strengthens public-private collaboration.

Areas of Contribution

- Participating in government advisory councils as industry representatives

- Spearheading advocacy campaigns with data-backed policy recommendations

- Promoting self-regulation norms showcasing feasibility and economic viability

- Supporting progressive policies through judicial interventions as expert facilitators

-

Civil Society Facilitation

Evidence-based Research and Policy Advisory

Civil society organizations (CSOs) play a key role in bridging knowledge gaps around air pollution through evidence-based studies analyzing trends, sources, health impacts, economic costs, global best practices and more. Such research provides data-backed advisory for governance improvements whether highlighting gaps in current emission inventories, pollution control infrastructure, scheme utilization, emergency response protocols etc.

For instance, Centre for Science and Environment's State of India's Environment Reports have authoritatively highlighted worsening particulate matter pollution across Indian cities - spotlighting pollution hotspots, seasonal variability, economic costs etc. while recommending mitigation pathways.

Awareness and Capacity Building

Leveraging their grassroot presence, CSOs run impactful public awareness and education campaigns around air quality - translating science, demystifying policy, busting myths and channeling outrage into constructive activism. Tailored capacity building of vulnerable communities also aids adoption of low-emission alternatives; whether training women self-help groups in clean cookstoves usage or demonstrating DIY air purifiers to schools in pollution hotspots.

CSOs similarly build capabilities of other stakeholders - from sensitizing doctors on latest pollution-health research for better diagnosis/counseling to building data monitoring capacities of resident welfare associations to highlight local pollution blackspots.

Bridging with Communities through Networks

Acting as vital liaisons between governments and citizens,

CSOs facilitate participatory governance around air quality management across cities and rural areas. Community engagement by CSOs has provided critical inputs to official planning processes - whether highlighting challenges faced by marginalized groups or providing hyperlocal solutions' ideas to state pollution control boards.

Some CSOs have also pioneered technology systems enabling transparent civic participation; from online portals allowing citizens to report air polluting activities in neighborhoods to mobile apps channeling public air quality complaints directly to responsible agencies.

Legal Activism and Public Interest Litigation

Impact litigation by environmental lawyers through PILs has proved pivotal in judiciary enforcing accountability from state and central governments around air quality governance failures. Landmark judgements due to such legal activism have expanded the ambit of Right to Life to include Right to Clean Air while directing time-bound pollution mitigation action across cities.

By upholding public interest and principles of natural justice, an activist judiciary has made environmental regulations more stringent; ensured greater accountability in policy implementation; and given a voice to future generations. Similar PIL activism has also helped protect communities impacted by industrial pollution such as in critically polluted industrial clusters.

Thus CSOs engage civil society to inform, advocate, mobilize and litigate across the ecology of institutions shaping air pollution discourse and decisions. Their multimodal facilitation amplifies public voices; co-creates localized solutions; enables participatory governance; and triggers accountability accelerating progress.

8.3 Healthcare Professionals

Deepening Understanding of Health Impacts

As first responders to pollution-exacerbated illnesses, healthcare professionals have a crucial role in furthering research on disease burdens to make the connections clearer for policymakers and public. Indian Medical Association's national studies quantifying impact of PM2.5 exposure on lung cancer, pregnancy complications etc. have been pivotal.

Research by pulmonologists into local pollution sources triggering asthma attacks or cardiologists isolating heart disease risks among traffic police personnel exposed to vehicular fumes provides more India-centric evidence. Transdisciplinary research collaboration between doctors, epidemiologists and pollution scientists also aids accelerate learnings.

Patient Counseling and Public Messaging

Given their unique community trust and respect, doctors also significantly shape public opinion around health risks especially for vulnerable patients through impactful counseling, awareness messaging and mainstream media outreach.

For instance leading doctors writing newspaper editorials ahead of Diwali urging usage of less polluting firecrackers or appearances on TV shows advising parents to minimize outdoor activity for children during severe smog episodes influences societal narratives significantly more than activism or policy announcements alone.

Advocacy within Medical Community

The medical community itself requires greater sensitization on latest environmental health research to diagnose and treat related illnesses better. Advocacy organizations like Doctors for Clean Air founded by healthcare experts spread awareness among medical fraternity through Continued Medical Education (CME) sessions.

Such efforts also collate pledged support from doctors for stronger air quality standards/enforcement and incorporation of environmental history in medical curriculum. Thereby advocacy groups enable healthcare community leadership to inform prevention and policy on the Sustainable Development Goal imperative of clean air.

Thus doctors as both healers and community influencers have twin responsibilities - to counsel and treat affected patients by deepening medical knowledge on pollution's health impacts while raising public risk awareness for societal momentum towards solutions. Their clinical and social advocacy thereby bridges vital gaps between pollution, health and governance.

8.4 Media Amplification

Consistent Narrative Building

Media plays a vital role in guiding public discourse and sustainably spotlighting air pollution amidst competing news cycles through data-driven storytelling. Long-form newspapers investigations analyzing trends across cities or opinion articles by eminent environmentalists connecting air quality to climate change or gender justice help consistently build narrative.

Even dedicated online explainers demystifying air quality terminology, index metrics evolution, health impacts etc. enables wider understanding. Thereby media enlarges the supporter base moving air pollution mitigation from niche environmental issue to mainstream civic problem affecting quality of life and economic growth.

Investigative Reportage and Campaigns

Field reportage highlighting granular ground realities also strengthens accountability. Whether investigating state data manipulation on pollution deaths, lack of emission compliance by industrial units or blackspots missed by official monitoring – such exposes jolt people and administration into remedial action.

Creative mediagenic campaigns like NDTV-CSE's Right to Breathe on rising respiratory ailments or podcast series like Blue Sky Thinking that put people living pollution hotspots at the center moves conversations from statistics to solutions.

Positive Storytelling on Innovations

Solutions journalism narrating stories of clean-tech innovations, localized heroes, policy wins etc. prevents issue fatigue and gives people agency. For instance, Times of India's Techie Tuesdays spotlighted startups building affordable air purifiers or low-cost sensors; while Quint profiled innovator developing pollution fighting black carbon ink.

Similarly, The Better India features hyperlocal changemakers leading community air quality monitoring and green drives in their cities. Such solutions showcase sparks mindset shift and scales what works. Thereby solutions-focused journalism seeds optimism and ideas for public-policy simulation.

Thus through narrativization, investigation and solutions spotlighting around air pollution, media reduces opacity; enhances accountability; centers people-impact; and propagates ideas that accelerate collaborative action binding citizens, cities and countries together for breathable futures

8.5 Cross-Country Case Studies

China's War on Pollution and Public-Private Collaboration

Faced with dangerously high air pollution levels, China demonstrated political will and policy prioritization by launching an expansive 'War on Pollution' campaign in 2014 that delivered remarkable turnaround within 5 years. This national mandate mobilized all levels of government and sectors using target-based performance management.

Central pollution inspectors were deputed to shame laggard cities while star performers were incentivized showcasing political commitment. Stringent industrial emission norms, coal usage limits and stiff penalties on violations also accessioned compliance from factories. Heavy investments into cleaner energy installations, public transit upgrades and pollution abatement infrastructure modernized urban sustainability.

China also fostered public-private partnerships facilitating market-based solutions. For instance, the government collaborated with IT giants Alibab and Tencent to develop nation-wide real-time air quality monitoring and online transparency portals that boosted civic participation. Such constructive state-corporate synergies enabled rapid scaleup of emerging technologies. Manufacturers were also encouraged to offer consumer appliances with air purification functionalities spurring market demand.

London's Congestion Charging Model and Citizen Engagement

London adopted a very citizen-centric approach for its pioneering Congestion Charging Scheme of 2003 which dramatically lowered central city traffic and emissions. Extensive public consultations informed scheme design through feedback incorporation on fee rates, operational hours, discounts etc. Telescopic surveys showcased likely personal mobility cost savings from modal shift to mass transit. Comprehensive multi-channel outreach campaigns educated people ahead on rules using media advertisements, direct mails and public demonstrations.

Post implementation, funds garnered were re-invested into improving bus services and cycling infrastructure as per people's preferences making the scheme politically acceptable. Ongoing citizen oversight committees continue advising enhancements accounting for emerging mobility solutions like EV adoption. This collaborative governance approach delivered positive outcomes building faith to expand the low emission zone geographically. London's participatory template has inspired many global cities for their congestion schemes putting people at the center.

Shenzhen's Electric Vehicle Ecosystem

The manufacturing hub of Shenzhen has created the world's largest electric fleet leveraging supportive regulations, financial incentives and public-private capabilities for accelerated adoption. Stringent license lotteries, purchase subsidies, HOV lane access etc. promoted EVs uptake. Collaborations with automakers guided R&D while association with power utilities bolstered charging infrastructure amplifying production and consumption.

Citizen engagement initiatives like subsiding residential setups and public test drive events promoted user readiness. Comprehensive policies also facilitated ecosystem expansion across EV manufacturing, battery recycling, mobility services and renewable energy integration. By fostering such synergistic opportunities, the Shenzhen model delivers sustainable scale at speed.

Thus these global case studies showcase the potency of multiparty orchestration across governments, businesses and civil society for air pollution mitigation anchored around ambitious targets, policies, financing mechanisms and civic participation. Blending top-down direction setting with collaborative governance and localized solutions can realize improved environmental sustainability.

CONCLUSIONS

Our Right to Breathe

Air pollution poses an existential public health and climate emergency threatening millions of lives across India while also severely denting economic growth prospects valued at 7-9% of GDP as per World Bank estimates.

Yet, the policy response has so far failed to match the devastating scale and urgency of this invisible killer. Piecemeal schemes remain underfunded without stringent accountability driving implementation gaps whether around emission compliance, pollution data transparency or health advisories.

Business as usual thus condemns India towards grim inequality trajectories where marginalized communities face amplified mortality risks just based on their misfortune of geography, income segments or social groups. This represents systemic prejudice against right to life and violates core constitutional principles of equality, justice and dignity.

But India stands at an inflection point today. An awakening generation of youth, armed with technologies, economic growth aspirations and intrinsic desire for better living conditions are voicing their dissent through activism, consumer choices, policies critiques and more. #RightToBreathe has become a clarion call for climate and social justice.

Channeling this momentum into constructive participation and accountability can catalyse a sustainability revolution transforming India into a global icon for climate leadership. The blueprint ideas across mobility innovations, renewable energy, emission regulation enforcement etc. discussed in earlier chapters aim to inform such a vision for change.

The Power of People

Central to this would be continued amplification of public voices, community participation and civic data to counter asymmetry of influence and enhance accountability.

Policy processes should institutionalize mechanisms for periodic inputs from citizens action groups while making all data open access. For instance, Beijing citizens vote on transportation priorities while Londoners co-create their neighborhoods emissions reduction plans.

Creative communication campaigns like Kenya's Shamba Shape Up edu-tainment show that inspires climate smart agriculture should be launched at scale on India's high-penetration entertainment platforms to sustain public engagement across geographies. Ultimately technology and media remain means, not saviors. People should direct technology usage.

Prudent Politics

India boasts strong institutional capabilities in government, bureaucracy and judiciary nurtured since independence. What is needed is redirection of political will across parties towards responsible governance upholding constitutional duties, especially around public health which should rise above partisan differences.

Convergence of policy priorities between center and states can deliver results as seen in aspirational flagships like Swachh Bharat Abhiyan. Inter-state competitions can promote collaborative learning. For instance, state government partnership with children helped Chhattisgarh outperform others in reducing Infant Mortality Rates.

Economies of Scale

India also needs to leverage latent economic opportunities around sustainability solutions job creation, import substitution, global leadership etc. Positioned as third largest energy consumer and home to widespread technology talent, India enjoys envious economies of scale to pioneer solutions where politically difficult pollution taxes can be skipped for market mechanisms kickstarting clean energy adoption.

Cross-sector collaboration around electric mobility between electricity utilities, battery manufacturers and ride sharing platforms can accelerate system level transformation. inviting sustainable FDI flows. Sound policies and incentives can unleash competitive forces making India the factory to the world for green products.

The Ethical Imperative

Most vitally though, discourse must elevate sustainability beyond technical metrics to questions of ethics and justice. Inter-generational theft perpetrated by unhindered ecological destruction fails principles of trusteeship. India's historical climate positioning advocating differentiated responsibilities and lifestyle sustainability should manifest locally.

Hence administrations need to transition from transactional pollution mitigation budgets to structural transformations reversing socio-economic inequities exacerbated by environmental degradation. Centre-state partnerships like Aspirational Districts Program improving healthcare, education etc. in marginalized pockets signify templates enabling pollution alleviation become means for wider change.

Our right to breathe hence also translates to breathing life into hopes, capabilities and liberties of our people. With youngest population worldwide, largest democracy upholding pluralism and festering injustices, India's policy choices will reverberate across the world this century as a civilizational model or warning sign. The alarm bells could not be louder. Public momentum never greater. Promise never more pregnant. Action can never be now. Destiny awaits to be written. Which side of history will we choose?

EPILOGUE

Epilogue: A Clear Vision for the Future

The battle to clear India's toxic skies has been engaged. Across cities and villages, people from all walks of life are waking up to the reality that purifying our air is not just an environmental issue, but an existential imperative that will define whether India flourishes or falters in the coming decades.

The road ahead will be immensely challenging, there is no denying that. Entrenched interests vested in the polluting status quo will not relent easily. Industries, power plants, and vehicles still spewing noxious fumes will need to make the costly transition to cleaner operations and technologies. Individual habits around burning solid fuels, waste disposal, and crop residue clearing must shift through a combination of regulation, incentives, and public awareness campaigns.

The administrative and financial capacity of central, state, and local governments will be strained in implementing and enforcing pollution control measures. Tax revenues, development budgets, and innovative financing instruments will all need to be channelled towards building out sustainable infrastructure and green public services. Corporations must reckon with their environmental balance sheets beyond just tokenistic corporate social responsibility gestures.

And most critically, the public consciousness around the urgency of clean air needs to be elevated and sustained beyond fleeting outrage over visibly smoggy days or viral images of shrunken skylines. Societal advocacy, legal action, and political accountability will all need ramping up until the culture of air pollution denial and apathy is permanently replaced with a culture of clean air awareness.

Make no mistake, the road ahead will be an intergenerational struggle akin to other protracted social and political transformations in the course of human civilization. But that should not dampen our resolve. For what could be more motivating than the prospect of handing over a nation with skies scrubbed of toxicity to today's children and future generations?

Think of an India where parents no longer have to fear for their kids' developing lungs with every breath. Where cities and villages are no longer shrouded in perpetual haze, but reveal their full splendid panoramas. Where the economic toll of pollution-related healthcare costs and productivity losses is reversed in favour of a robust, sustainable growth trajectory. Where no quarter of society - rich or poor, rural or urban - bears disproportionate impacts, but all citizens enjoy their birthrights to clean air and healthy living equally.

This is the soaring vision that has been cast in this book and that we must collectively strive to make real through concerted multi-stakeholder action and a true whole-of-society commitment. There is no convenient shortcut, but each action toward cleaning our skies - however incremental it may seem in isolation - lays another brick in the foundation of the blue future we're building.

So let this book be the trumpet that has sounded the charge for us all to join the battle. To the bureaucrats, industrialists, and government ministers with authority and capital to catalyse change at scale - your resolve and resources are needed more than ever before. To the citizens, activists, and advocacy groups with righteous grit and moral clarity - your voices and mobilizing spirit must never be stilled until the final victory over smog is sealed.

And to the youth inheriting this crisis - find purpose in the struggle, voice, and vision articulated in this book. For only your generation's unwavering urgency can write the epilogue of this chapter as not a tragic tale of planetary plunder, but an inspiring testament to human grit in overcoming what seemed like insurmountable odds and bequeathing a gift of clean air to all of posterity.

The fight will be arduous, but the rewards greater than any riches money can buy. For what wealth can compensate for tainted lungs or shortened lifespans? What prosperity can be built on foundations of ill health and environmental destruction?

Clean, breathable air is the most precious resource - the source code of life itself. May this book be the guiding star that aligns all efforts toward that most sacred pursuit. With unified commitment, the soaring vision of azure Indian skies is ours to make real. Future generations are watching, and history will render its judgment on whether we had the foresight and fortitude to course-correct before it was too late.

REFERENCES

Air Quality Life Index (AQLI) (2022). Air Quality Life Index (AQLI) Annual Update. University of Chicago. Retrieved from https://aqli.epic.uchicago.edu/reports/

Balakrishnan, K., Dey, S., Gupta, T., Dhaliwal, R.S., Brauer, M., Cohen, A.J., Stanaway, J.D., Beig, G., Joshi, T.K., Aggarwal, A.N., Sabde, Y., Sadhu, H., Frostad, J., Causey, K., Godakandage, S.S., Acharya, P., Chaterjee, P., Bhansali, S., Rana, U., ... Dandona, L. (2019). The impact of air pollution on deaths, disease burden, and life expectancy across the states of India: The Global Burden of Disease Study 2017. The Lancet Planetary Health, 3(1), e26-e39. https://doi.org/10.1016/S2542-5196(18)30261-4

Centre for Science and Environment (CSE) (2022). State of India's Environment 2022. Retrieved from https://www.cseindia.org/state-of-india-s-environment-10498

Health Effects Institute (HEI) (2019). State of Global Air 2019. Special Report. Retrieved from https://www.stateofglobalair.org/resources/global-air-2019

IQAir (2022). World Air Quality Report 2022. Retrieved from https://www.iqair.com/world-air-quality-report

Krishnan, S., Currais, L., Nataraj, S., & Saldiva, P.H.N. (2022). Air pollution and health expenditures: A comparative study for Brazil, India and Mexico. Environment International, 159, 107011. https://doi.org/10.1016/j.envint.2021.107011

Ravindra, K., Singh, T., Pandey, V., & Mor, S. (2022). Air Pollution in India: An Introduction. In Air Pollution in India: Sources,

Impacts and Management (pp. 1-24). Springer, Singapore. https://doi.org/10.1007/978-981-19-0688-9_1

World Health Organization (WHO) (2021). WHO global air quality guidelines: particulate matter (PM2.5 and PM10), ozone, nitrogen dioxide, sulfur dioxide and carbon monoxide. Retrieved from https://apps.who.int/iris/handle/10665/345329

Central Pollution Control Board (CPCB) (2019). National Clean Air Programme. Retrieved from https://cpcb.nic.in/uploads/National_Clean_Air_Programme.pdf

Central Pollution Control Board (CPCB) (2021). Continuous Emission Monitoring Systems (CEMS) for Monitoring of Pollutants from Stationary Sources. Retrieved from https://cpcb.nic.in/cems/

Jitendra (2021, November 29). National Green Tribunal orders 8 states to ensure zero stubble burning. Down To Earth. Retrieved from https://www.downtoearth.org.in/news/pollution/national-green-tribunal-orders-8-states-to-ensure-zero-stubble-burning-80437

Ministry of Environment, Forest and Climate Change (MoEFCC) (2015). Revised Emission Norms for Thermal Power Plants. Retrieved from https://moef.gov.in/wp-content/uploads/2017/11/thermal_plant_2015.pdf

Ministry of Environment, Forest and Climate Change (MoEFCC) (2020). National Clean Air Programme (NCAP). Retrieved from https://moef.gov.in/wp-content/uploads/2020/03/NCAP_Report.pdf

Ministry of Road Transport and Highways (MoRTH) (2020). Introduction of BS-VI Emission Norms in India. Retrieved from https://pib.gov.in/PressReleasePage.aspx?PRID=1604587

National Green Tribunal (NGT) (2021, November 29). Order in Original Application No. 1038/2019. Retrieved from https://

greentribunal.gov.in/sites/default/files/orders/2021/11/nn/
original_application_no._1038_of_2019_dated_29.11.2021.pdf

Supreme Court of India (2018, October 29). Order in M.C. Mehta vs
Union Of India & Ors. Retrieved from https://indiankanoon.org/
doc/23357029/

Central Pollution Control Board (CPCB) (2021). National Clean
Air Programme (NCAP) India. Retrieved from https://cpcb.nic.in/
uploads/National_Clean_Air_Programme.pdf

China Biogas (n.d.). Rural Biogas Development in China. Retrieved
from   https://biogas.ifri.org/site/uploads/biogaz/biogaz/1/
china_biogas_project.pdf

Delhi Metro Rail Corporation (DMRC) (2022). Delhi Metro
Network. Retrieved from https://www.delhimetrorail.com/
network-map/

International Energy Agency (IEA) (2022). India Energy Outlook
2022. Retrieved from https://www.iea.org/reports/india-energy-
outlook-2022

Ministry of Environment, Forest and Climate Change (MoEFCC)
(2022). Annual Report 2021-22. Retrieved from https://
moef.gov.in/wp-content/uploads/2022/03/Annual-
Report-2021-22-English.pdf

Ministry of New and Renewable Energy (MNRE) (2022). Rooftop
Solar Programme Phase II. Retrieved from https://mnre.gov.in/
solar/schemes/

Ministry of Road Transport and Highways (MoRTH) (2022).
Annual Report 2021-22. Retrieved from https://morth.gov.in/
sites/default/files/documents/English.pdf

National Green Tribunal (NGT) (2021, November 29). Order in
Original Application No. 1038/2019. Retrieved from https://
greentribunal.gov.in/sites/default/files/orders/2021/11/nn/

original_application_no._1038_of_2019_dated_29.11.2021.pdf

Niti Aayog (2021). Roadmap for Ethanol Blending in India 2020-25. Retrieved from https://niti.gov.in/sites/default/files/2021-06/EthanolBlendingInIndia_successes_roadmap_docs_01062021.pdf

United Nations Development Programme (UNDP) (2022). Sustainable Cities in India. Retrieved from https://www.in.undp.org/content/india/en/home/sustainable-development/sustainable-cities.html

Unnikrishnan, S., & Singh, M. (2022, January 10). NITI Aayog pushes for more biomass plants in rural areas. The Economic Times. Retrieved from https://economictimes.indiatimes.com/industry/energy/power/niti-aayog-pushes-for-more-biomass-plants-in-rural-areas/articleshow/88821631.cms

World Bank (2022). India: Country Environmental Analysis. Retrieved from https://openknowledge.worldbank.org/handle/10986/36613

ABOUT THE AUTHOR

Naresh Garg

Naresh Garg is a passionate advocate for environmental protection whose multi-faceted career has given him a unique perspective on India's air pollution crisis.

Garg's academic training includes a Bachelor of Science degree and a Master of Science in Environmental Sciences, where he was a UGC-NET qualified scholar. This robust scientific foundation has allowed him to analyse the root causes and impacts of air pollution through an empirical, data-driven lens.

However, Garg's expertise extends far beyond the classroom. He has worked in the trenches at a thermal electricity power plant, witnessing firsthand the environmental degradation caused by fossil fuel combustion. He has conducted research at an environmental science laboratory, studying pollution mitigation technologies and modelling air quality scenarios.

Garg has also been an educator. This experience fostering environmental literacy in young minds underscored both the urgency of the crisis and the importance of raising public awareness across generations.

In addition to his core professional roles, Garg has volunteered and consulted for numerous environmental non-profits and advocacy groups working to clear India's skies. He has participated in many initiatives launched by the Central Pollution Control Board (CPCB), World Wide Fund for Nature (WWF) India, United Nations Environment Programme (UNEP), and the Centre for Science and Environment (CSE).

At the grassroots level, Garg has collaborated with local citizen groups in his hometown of Delhi to campaign for clean air action plans and compliance enforcement on polluters. He is also a practicing astrologer, blending his scientific training with India's ancient spiritual traditions to offer a holistic, cosmic perspective on humanity's relationship with the environment.

Garg's diverse experiences across sectors have coalesced into an unshakeable commitment to using every tool at his disposal - from rigorous empirical research to impassioned activism - to solve the air pollution public health emergency.

This book represents the culmination of over a decade of learning, researching, teaching, campaigning and lived experiences related to India's pollution crisis. Woven through its pages is Sharma's fervent hope that the knowledge and policy solutions compiled can catalyse coordinated action to bequeath the precious inheritance of clean air to all citizens and future generations.

Most critically, Garg aims to universally reframe India's mind-set - from perceiving pollution as an unavoidable byproduct of development, to recognizing environmental stewardship as a moral and existential imperative. Only then can the nation's skies be reclaimed as thriving azure habitats rather than hazardous human health threats.